CALIFORNIA
REVIVAL KNITS

CALIFORNIA
REVIVAL KNITS

Stephannie Tallent

COOPERATIVE PRESS
Cleveland, Ohio

Library of Congress Control Number: 2012936652
ISBN 13: 978-1-937513-06-1
First Edition
Published by Cooperative Press
http://www.cooperativepress.com

Patterns, charts and text © 2012, Stephannie Tallent
Photos © 2012, Kathy Cadigan
Adamson House photos pages 14 and 15 courtesy of the Malibu Lagoon Museum Archives

Models: Kristi Porter, Stephannie Tallent, Morgan Cadigan, Susan Moskwa, Obi the cat

Every effort has been made to ensure that all the information in this book is accurate at the time of publication, however Cooperative Press neither endorses nor guarantees the content of external links referenced in this book.

If you have questions or comments about this book, or need information about licensing, custom editions, special sales, or academic/corporate purchases, please contact Cooperative Press: info@cooperativepress.com or 13000 Athens Ave C288, Lakewood, OH 44107 USA

FOR COOPERATIVE PRESS

Senior Editor: Shannon Okey
Technical Editor: Alexandra Virgiel
Assistant Editor: Elizabeth Green Musselman

SPECIAL THANKS

Sample knitters: Ellen Stratton (knitdesignsbyelle.com), Jamie Hess
Test knitters: Amanda Bell, Claudine Alderete, Ellen Stratton, Jamie Hess, Sarah and zuzon58
Charting software: Envisioknit

TO DAVE—I COULDN'T HAVE DONE THIS WITHOUT YOU

AND TO MY MOM & DAD, CAROLE AND PAUL,
AS WELL AS MY IN-LAWS,
ROSEMARY AND CURTIS—MY BIGGEST FANS

Table of Contents

Peacock Mitts, 17

Peacock Cowl, 25

Tiles Sweater, 29

Peacock Shawl, 37

UnderSea Garden Cowl, 41

Stair Steps Tam, 45

INTRODUCTION

Old houses have always appealed to me. Clichéd as it is, they really do have more character in their bones, even a small kit house by the beach such as ours, than most modern homes. When we decided to sell our first home, we knew we wanted a bungalow of some sort. And we really wanted a California Revival bungalow.

After the Arts & Crafts movement of the early 'teens, various 'revival styles' grabbed the fancy of the public. Tudor, Pueblo, Mission, Spanish Colonial, Spanish Revival, and Cottage were among the different styles being adapted to then-modern living. If you wander through the older neighborhoods, such as Belmont Heights, of Long Beach, California, you'll see lovingly restored Tudor bungalows next to older Craftsmen bungalows, sandwiched in between Spanish Revival bungalows. Note that when I'm talking about older neighborhoods, or historical architecture, I'm talking in California terms; so although you'll find Victorians in, say, San Francisco, the majority of 'old houses' in California are going to be Craftsman (1905-1919) and Revival style houses (1920s).

To me, California Revival can include Mission, Spanish Colonial or Spanish Revival styles; at a certain point, unless you're a historical architectural scholar, the differences are very tiny. Regardless, all those styles feature stucco, red tile roofs, coved ceilings, tile, tile, and more tile (with Spanish, Moorish or Mexican influences) and wrought iron. How elaborate the house is depends of course on the wealth of the original occupants—think Hearst Castle versus the typical Californian casita.

We found our California Revival bungalow in Hermosa Beach. Hermosa Beach, unfortunately, doesn't support its historic houses or neighborhoods, so there aren't many of these houses left. Most are considered tear downs. We were lucky that this one was for sale when we were house hunting.

It's only had a handful of owners, and luckily, no character-removing renovations. It's one of six or seven bungalows in a small area, and sits on an oddly-shaped corner lot; we have a relatively large front yard, which we landscaped ourselves with California native plants and some fruit trees, and a backyard that's not even really big enough to be considered a side yard by most people's standards.

However, with its oak floors, curved and coved ceilings, and logical layout, our home is cozy and welcoming. Granted, it does have very small closets, only one small bathroom, and really not enough kitchen counter or cupboard space, even including the vintage Hoosier cabinet. But it's certainly enough for me, my husband Dave, our cats (Meggie, Cali and Obi), and our dog Rigel. Within its 900 or so square feet are enough walls for all our bookcases, a nook for our daybed off the dining room, and a small space in the laundry room for our desk, computer and printer—with a peek view of the ocean.

With our acquisition of our home, I threw myself into learning about its style. Although the house hadn't had any bad renovations, after nearly 90 years of existence, it is due for kitchen and bath renovations. However, we want to keep any renovations within the style of the house. I started collecting books on bungalows in general and on the California Revival style, in particular. I've listed these books in the bibliography for you.

Adamson House

We also started paying attention to houses in historical districts. Little surprise that one of my favorite houses I've toured is the Adamson House in Malibu. Built around the same time as our modest house, the Adamson House features all of the details you'd expect and treasure in a showpiece California Revival house of the period. The tilework, of course, is the main feature—the owner of the house was the daughter of May Rindge, who established Malibu Potteries in the late 1920s.

The details in the tiles, from the amazing fringed Persian rug in the hallway, to the fully tiled upstairs bathrooms, to the exterior turquoise and light jade green peacock fountain, is wondrous.

Both the colors and designs supply a wellspring of inspiration. In fact, the colors of this collection—turquoise, jade green, cream, rich brown, deep red, cobalt blue—are directly inspired by the colors of the tiles. Many of the motifs are as well, of course, especially in the color work patterns.

The counterpoint to the colors and strong graphics of the tiles are the swoops, curls and lines of the ubiquitous iron used in gates, grates, stair railings and more. The Wrought projects, with their strong vertical twisted stitch lines punctuated by curved travelling stitches, hearken to wrought iron pieces. The Quatrefoil mitts use the quatrefoil pattern commonly found on iron grates, lamp shades, and screens.

California Potteries

Catalina Tileworks and Malibu Potteries were two of the best known potteries of the 1920s and '30s, but perusal of the various tile books (see bibliography) reveals a plethora of different companies.

Several companies today utilize the traditional tile making steps to create both new and reproduction designs. California Pottery and Tile Works is the largest of these, with clients ranging from local

homeowners restoring their homes to the city of Santa Barbara to Disney.

Conrad took me for a tour of the factory, located in south central Los Angeles. Each meticulous step of the process of creating the tiles is monitored or done by hand, from pressing out the clay, to creating then silkscreening the design on the tiles, to the painting 'by numbers', then the final glazing and subsequent inspection. The process is both mechanized (presses for the tiles, for example, that flatten the initial lump of clay into a small sheet of imprinted squares, to be hand cut later) and intensely hands-on; even the field, or solid, tiles (patterned tiles are deco tiles) are handcrafted.

They have a stock range of colors, but also will match colors. Because the tiles are generally made to order, you can request your own color scheme. They can also 'age' tiles to match existing, installed tiles (or just to make the installation look like it was set in place in the 1920s).

It's the antithesis to the mass-produced, overconsumption of our time.

In pulling inspiration from a style that flourished 80 years ago I've tried to link my personal craft, knitting, to the craftsmanship of that time that I so admire. I do hope I've succeeded. Take your time with the projects, savoring the process of creating something beautiful.

THE DESIGN PROCESS

How did I get from, say, a tiled Persian rug to socks with bicolored cables? Or even the idea that tiles and wrought iron could be translated to knitting?

I knew I wanted to do a collection unified by color and theme. I initially thought I'd do just a small ebook, with just a few designs, incorporating the colors and motifs of the architectural style I love, so I started working on a mood board.

When I first started designing, and looking at calls for submissions, one of the many things I learned about was mood boards: a composite of images, text, and color swatches meant to evoke the theme of the final magazine story, book, or pattern collection. Creating mood boards for my own collections is now one of my favorite parts of the process.

For this book, I began seeking images from the period and of architectural details that fit into the style. I scoured the books in my personal library for images that resonated. I checked out books from our local public libraries. Anything that seemed remotely interesting or usable I tagged, bookmarked, sketched, clipped, or just let sink in. Anything digital went into my mood board or just saved in a folder on my laptop. If I'd been using Pinterest more at the time, I'd have pinned more images (as it is, I only have a couple small boards there related to this book).

I began developing twisted stitch and colorwork motifs based on the images I found. I originally thought I'd do cables, too, but ended up wanting to do just twisted stitches. You can just get more movement out of them on a small canvas. I also began digging through my library for stitch patterns that fit my vision of the theme. I did lots of charting.

 At the same time, I decided what types of patterns I wanted: sweaters, socks, mitts, hats, and so on, and what motifs I wanted to used for each. I began swatching the various motifs. I began looking for yarn to match the growing pattern list. I knew, for the most part, that I wanted to work with indie or small yarn companies. I studied their bases and colorways. I created proposals including a bit about the collection, the colorways, and the specific piece I wanted to do with each company's yarn.

I also decided on a color palette: colors from the tiles themselves. Turquoise, red, jade, cream, brown, cobalt…

It made sense to me that the tile-inspired patterns would play more with color, and the wrought iron patterns with texture, but there is a little bit of crossover, primarily with the Quatrefoil mitts. The lace patterns were also primarily tile-inspired, but more by motifs, or themes, than colors. The Peacock mitts and cowl are the most literal of the patterns, incorporating intarsia and duplicate stitch, which gives the most allowance for that sort of depiction.

And the Fringe socks? I was so taken by that Persian rug of tiles when I toured the Adamson House for the first time. It was one of my favorite things I saw. I just loved the trompe l'oeil effect of flowing fringe depicting in clay tile. I wanted to depict something that looked like fringe, but wasn't, just like those tiles. I finally decided on semi-random bicolored cables, knit stitches upon a knit background (purl just didn't work as well). Which way to point them? I originally had them flowing from corrugated ribbing, but didn't really like the corrugating ribbing for socks; and what else to do for the rest of the sock? Just fringe seemed too boring. Another iteration had a ribbed cuff, the fringe, then the rest of the sock in stranded stockinette, patterned over the entire sock; but having the fringe point up didn't make sense to me. I finally decided on main color ribbed cuff, then a combination of stranded knitting and braids—to evoke the edge of a rug—then the fringe, then the remainder of the sock in simple stockinette, taking advantage of the rich color of the yarn.

PEACOCK MITTS

The Peacock Cowl and Peacock Mitts are inspired by the gorgeous peacock fountains that abound in the designs of the California Revival.

Both mitts are initially worked in intarsia, using only three colors: the base color, the base peacock color, and the base flower color. After the base piece is finished, block it, then work the duplicate stitch embroidery.

Sit down with a cup of coffee or tea and take your time! Start with the flowers; they're easier, and if this is your first time duplicate stitching, you'll get plenty of practice before starting the peacock. With the peacock, while you should be precise with the eye, beak, neck and legs duplicate stitching, you can use the chart as a guideline for the tail and body highlights and the feather embroidery.

I wanted to highlight the different Shetland yarns, and chose to make two different colorways. The teal and fuchsia colorway of the cowl evokes the bright colors of many of the fountains I've seen; the blue colorway of the mitts is more subtle.

Size: One

Finished Measurements
8in / 20.5cm hand circumference, 9in / 23cm tall

Yarn
Elemental Affects Natural Shetland Fingering, 115 yds / 28g, 2 skeins in Mioget (MC) and 1 ball each in the following colors:

- Violet (main color flowers) (IC)
- Denim (main color peacock body) (IC)
- Teal (peacock tail eye center) (DPC)
- Lichen (peacock tail eye outer color) (DPC)
- Aegean Sea (peacock body & wing details) (DPC)
- Pumpkin (peacock legs, beak) (DPC)
- Scarlet (peacock eye) (DPC)
- Periwinkle (edge flowers) (DPC)
- Moorit (tree branch) (DPC)

Please note for the duplicate stitching you need less than 20 yards of each duplicate stitch color (DPC). Intarsia colors are noted by (IC). Kits for these mitts including all colors needed, beads and buttons are available through Elemental Affects, www.elementalaffects.com

Needles
US size 0 (2mm) or size to obtain gauge.

Gauge
28 sts and 44 rnds = 4in/ 10cm in stockinette stitch

Notions & Other Supplies
Extra needle or waste yarn for provisional cast on
Tiny crochet hook for beading (I use a size .8mm steel hook)
Yarn needle
24 small (¼") pearl buttons. Buttons shown are JHB #11280.
24in / 60cm ½"grosgrain or velvet ribbon for trim, coordinating thread and sewing needle (optional)
Stitch markers as desired

Beads
Size 6/0 for flower centers (18), peacock eye (2), and peacock feathers (22). Beads used from www.beadwrangler.com (approx 480 beads/tube); #s 656 & 612 for flowers, #404 for eyes, #721 for peacock feathers. I highly recommend purchasing more beads than this quantity to account for breakage, loss, etc.

Required Skills
Beading, picot hems, provisional cast on, sewn hem.

HOW TO PLACE BEADS

- Work up to the stitch that will have a bead.
- Place the bead onto the crochet hook.
- Grab the stitch on the left hand needle with the hook. I pull tightly so that the yarn is as snug as possible against the crochet hook.
- Pull the bead over the yarn. You should have a loop of yarn— the stitch—sticking out of the bead.
- Replace the stitch onto the left hand needle. The bead is sitting below the knitting needle.
- Knit the stitch.

Instructions
Picot Hem
With MC, provisionally cast on 66 stitches. Work 6 rows in St st, beg with a RS row.
Picot row (RS): *Yo, k2tog; rep from * to end.
Work 6 more rows in St st.
Hem row (WS): Place sts from provisional CO onto a spare needle.

Fold hem with wrong sides together, spare needle in front of working needle. *K1 from front needle tog with 1 from back needle; rep from * to end.

Hand
Next row (RS): Using the knitted cast on, cast on 4 sts. [K1, p1] twice, then begin working first row of the Right or Left mitt base chart. Turn.
Row 2 (WS): Using the knitted cast on, cast on 4 sts. P2, k1, p1, then work the second row of the chart to 4 sts from end, p1, k1, p2.
Row 3: Sl1wyib, p1, k1, p1, work chart, [p1, k1] twice.
Row 4: Sl1wyif, p1, k1, p1, work chart, p1, k1, p2.
Right Mitt: Row 5 (RS buttonhole row): Sl1wyib, p1, yo, p2tog, work in established pattern to end.
Left Mitt: Row 5 (RS buttonhole row): Work in established pattern

to 4 sts before end, p2tog, yo, p1, k1.
Continue in established pattern until Row 12.

Right Mitt: Row 12 (WS buttonhole row): Work in established pattern to 4 sts before end, p2tog, yo, p2.
Left Mitt: Row 12 (WS buttonhole row): Sl1wyif, p1, yo, p2tog, work in established pattern to end.
Continue in established pattern, working decreases and buttonhole rows as charted, through Row 38.
Begin Thumb Gusset on Row 39 as follows (RS): Work in pattern to bordered sts, pm, m1r, k2, m1L, pm, work in pattern to end.
Next row (WS): Work in pattern to marker, sm, purl to next marker, slip marker, work in pattern to end.
Next row: Work in pattern to marker, sm, m1R, knit to next marker, m1L, sm, work in pattern to end.
Repeat last 2 rows until you have 24 sts between markers. Work even for 7 rows. Next row (RS): Work to marker, remove marker, k3, place next 18 sts on waste yarn, using backward loop method CO 2 sts, k3, remove marker, work in pattern to end.
Complete chart.
Next row (RS): BO 4 sts knitwise, purl to 4 sts before end, p1, k1, p2.
Next row (WS): BO 4 sts purlwise, purl to end.

Top Picot Hem
Work 4 more rows in St st.
Picot row (RS): *Yo, k2tog; rep from * to end.
Work 5 more rows in St st. Fold hem with wrong sides facing and sew live sts down.

Thumb
Place gusset sts onto needles. Pick up 2 sts from of edge of opening, then knit across gusset sts. PM for beg of rnd. Knit 1 rnd. Purl 1 rnd. Knit 4 rnds.
Picot rnd (RS): *Yo, k2tog; rep from * to end.
Knit 5 rnds. Sew hem as above.

Finishing
Duplicate stitch as indicated on the duplicate stitch chart.
Sew beads as follows if you have not chosen to place them as you go along.
For peacock eye, sew red bead over Scarlet.
For tail feather beads, sew at center of Teal stitches.
Sew buttons. Weave in all ends. Block. Sew grosgrain or velvet ribbon under button band (side with buttons) if desired.

Left Mitt: Base

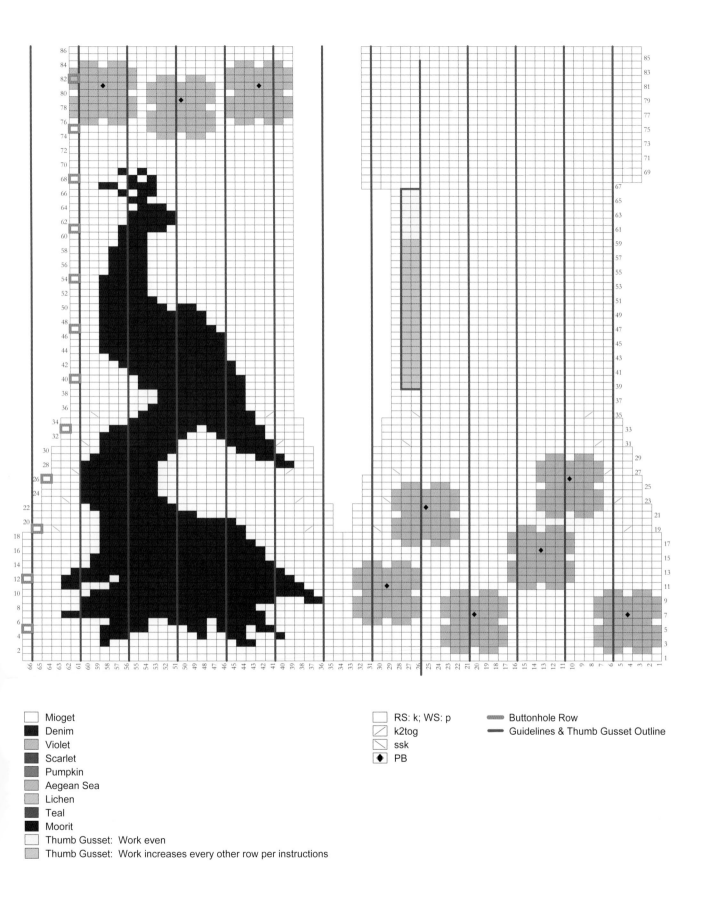

Mioget

Denim

Violet

Scarlet

Pumpkin

Aegean Sea

Lichen

Teal

Moorit

Thumb Gusset: Work even

Thumb Gusset: Work increases every other row per instructions

RS: k; WS: p

k2tog

ssk

PB

Buttonhole Row

Guidelines & Thumb Gusset Outline

Left Mitt: Duplicate Stitch Guide

 Denim
Mioget
Violet
Periwinkle
Moorit
Lichen
Teal
Aegean Sea
Pumpkin
Scarlet

RIGHT MITT: BASE

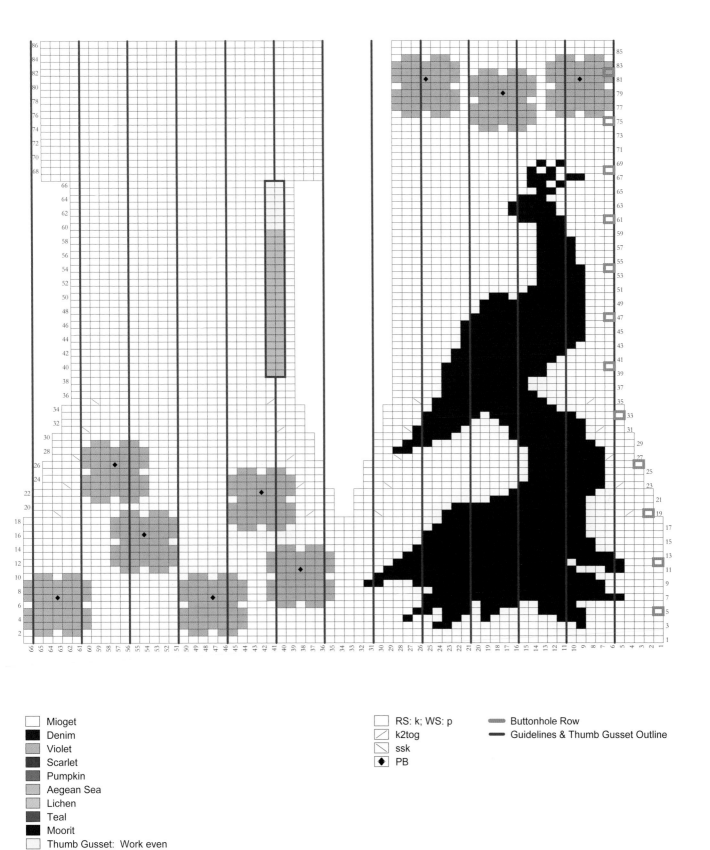

Mioget
Denim
Violet
Scarlet
Pumpkin
Aegean Sea
Lichen
Teal
Moorit
Thumb Gusset: Work even
Thumb Gusset: Work increases every other row per instructions

RS: k; WS: p
k2tog
ssk
PB

Buttonhole Row
Guidelines & Thumb Gusset Outline

Denim
Mioget
Violet
Periwinkle
Moorit
Lichen
Teal
Aegean Sea
Pumpkin
Scarlet

PEACOCK COWL

Size: One size

Finished Measurements
Approx 9¾in / 25cm tall, 23in / 58.5cm circumference

Yarn
Jamieson's Shetland Spindrift, 100% Shetland wool, 115 yds/ 25 gr ball, 2 balls in Ivory (MC) and 1 ball each in the following colors:
- Espresso
- Nighthawk
- Fuchsia
- Crimson
- Buttercup
- Rust
- Jade
- Gentian
- Caspian

Needles
US size 1 (2.25mm) or size to obtain gauge

Gauge
28 sts and 44 rows = 4in / 10cm in stockinette stitch

Notions & Other Supplies
Extra needle or waste yarn for provisional cast on
Crochet hook for beading, see directions page 17.
Yarn needle
Beads Size 6/0 for flower centers (57), peacock eye (4), and peacock feathers (40). Beads used from www.beadwrangler.com (approx 480 beads/tube); #s 721 for flowers, #404 for eyes, #612 for peacock feathers. I highly recommend purchasing more beads than this quantity to account for breakage, loss, etc.
13 small pearl buttons. Buttons shown are JHB #11280.
10in / 25cm of grosgrain or velvet ribbon ½in wide (optional)
Fabric to line cowl (optional)

Skills Required
Beading, picot hems, provisional cast on, sewn hem, intarsia, stranded knitting

Pattern Notes
Work Chart Rows 2-16 and 79-93 in stranded knitting, rather than intarsia.
The green outlined stiches simply indicate this is a buttonhole row.

Picot Hem
With MC, provisionally cast on 149 sts.
K 1 row with MC. Change to CC of choice for inner hem and work 7 more rows St st.
Change to MC.
Picot row (RS): *K2tog, yo; rep from * to 1 st before end, k1.
Cont in St st for a further 8 rows.
Hem row (WS): Place sts from provisional CO onto a spare needle.

Fold hem with wrong sides together, spare needle in front of working needle. *K1 from front needle tog with 1 from back needle; rep from * to end.

Main Body of Cowl
Row 1 (RS): Using the knitted cast on, cast on 6 sts. [K1, p1] 3 times, then work first row of Base Chart.
Row 2 (WS): Cast on 6 sts. P2, [k1, p1] 2 times, then work the second row of the chart. [P1, k1] 2 times, p2.
Row 3: Sl1wyib, p1, [k1, p1] twice, work chart, [p1, k1] 3 times.
Row 4: Sl1wyif, p1, [k1, p1] twice, work chart, [p1, k1] twice, p2.
Row 5: Repeat Row 3.
Row 6 (WS buttonhole row): Work in established pattern to last 6 sts. P1, k2tog, yo, k1, p2.
Continue in established pattern until Row 13.
Row 13 (RS buttonhole row): Sl1wyib, p1, k1, yo, k2tog, p1, work in established pattern to end.
Continue in established pattern, working buttonhole every 7th row, through end of chart (94 rows).

Top Hem
Next row (RS): BO 6 sts knitwise, purl to 6 sts before end, [p1, k1] 3 times.
Next row (WS): BO 6 sts purlwise, purl to end.
Work 6 rows in St st, beg with a knit row.
Picot row (RS): *K2tog, yo; rep from * to 1 st before end, k1.
Work 7 rows in St st with CC, as for lower hem. Change to MC and work 1 more row.
Fold hem with wrong sides together and sew live stitches down.

Finishing
Weave in all ends. Block.
Duplicate stitch as indicated on the duplicate stitch chart. Note that you should be precise with the placement of the stitching for the flowers, branches, eye, beak and feet/legs, but you can use the chart as a guideline for the rest of the peacock.
Sew one blue bead per peacock feather "eye." Sew red bead for actual peacock eyes.
Sew on buttons.
Sew grosgrain or velvet ribbon under button band (side with buttons) if desired. Line WS of cowl with fabric if desired.

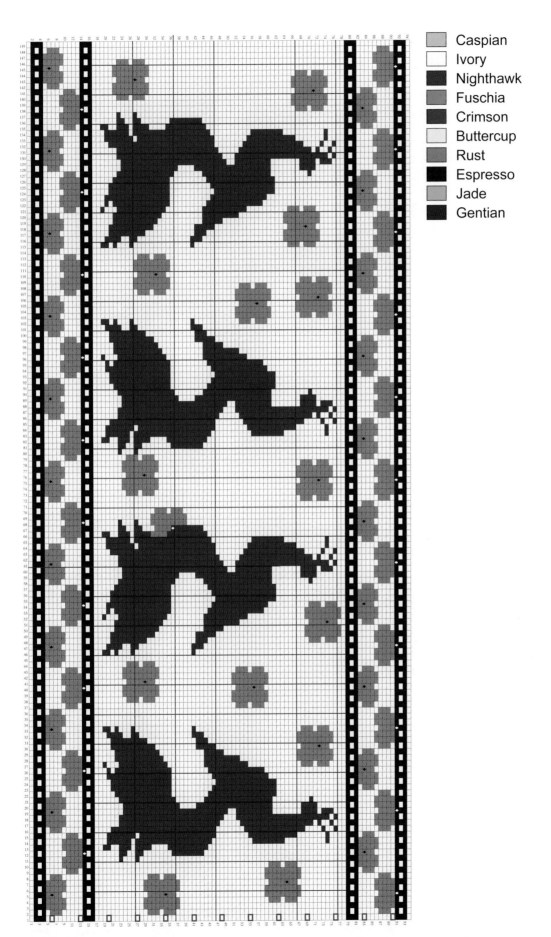

Caspian
Ivory
Nighthawk
Fuschia
Crimson
Buttercup
Rust
Espresso
Jade
Gentian

RS: k; WS: p
PB

Buttonhole Row
Guidelines

Duplicate Stitch Guide

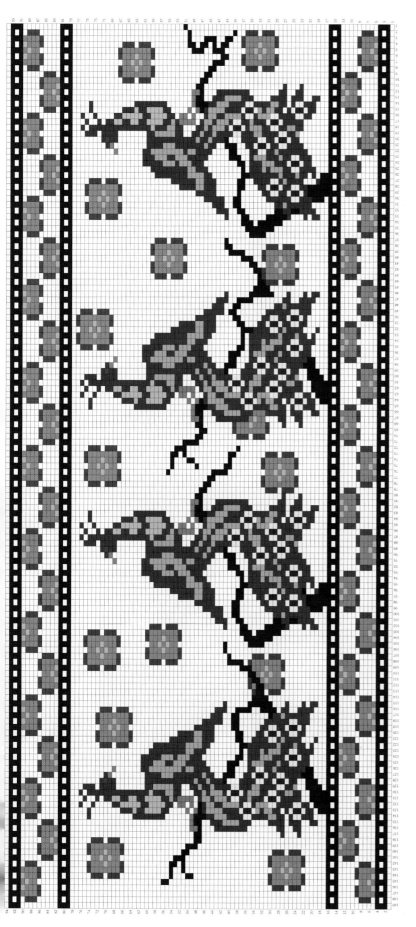

Caspian
Ivory
Nighthawk
Fuschia
Crimson
Buttercup
Rust
Espresso
Jade
Gentian

TILES SWEATER

I've grown to love beadwork. The motifs in this sweater are meant to evoke the simple Moroccan geometric shapes that you find in many of the deco (decorated) tiles.

The silk/merino/cashmere yarn from Woolen Rabbit makes a lovely, soft, warm but lightweight fabric with wonderful drape; no wonder it's Opal Kim's (the dyer's) go-to sweater yarn. The sweater is shown with an inch or two of ease, with figure-flattering shaping in the form of front and back darts.

Size
XS (S, M, L, XL, 2X, 3X)
Intended to be worn with 2-2½in / 5-6cm of ease.

Finished Measurements
Bust 30¼ (35, 37½, 42½, 47½, 49¾, 54¾)in / 75.5 (87.5, 94, 106, 118.5, 124.5, 137)cm

Yarn
Woolen Rabbit Opal, 75% merino/15% silk/10% cashmere, 415 yds / 115g, 4 (4, 5, 5, 6, 6, 7) skeins in Godiva

Needles
US 3 (3.25mm): long circular for body and circular(s)/double pointed for sleeves.
US 2½ (3mm): long circular for body and circular(s)/double pointed for sleeves and neck edging.
.8mm steel crochet hook

Gauge
26 sts and 40 rnds = 4in / 10cm in stockinette stitch with larger needles.

Notions & Other Supplies
Waste yarn, 6 stitch markers, tiny crochet hook for beading, yarn needle.
Beads size 6/0 from www.beadwrangler.com (approx 480 beads/tube)
#107 Egg Shell 617 (660, 699, 783, 839, 889, 941) beads
#456 Dk Red Luster OP 356 (384, 408, 460, 496, 528, 560) beads
#721 Emerald Rbw 58 (63, 66, 74, 80, 84, 88) beads
I highly recommend purchasing more beads than this quantity to account for breakage, loss, etc.

Required Skills
Knitting in the round, beading, picot hems, sewn hems, provisional cast on, 3 needle bind off.

Pattern Notes
There are three sections in which you can make the body of the sweater (from armholes to hem) longer. The first is immediately after the border; knit additional rounds as desired prior to beginning waist shaping. The second is after the waist decreases but before the bust increases. The last is after the bust increases but prior to beginning the neckline chart.

Row gauge is important for placement of beading. Please check your row gauge and adjust where you begin beading, if needed.

HOW TO PLACE BEADS

- Work up to the stitch that will have a bead.
- Place the bead onto the crochet hook.
- Grab the stitch on the left hand needle with the hook. I pull tightly so that the yarn is as snug as possible against the crochet hook.
- Pull the bead over the yarn. You should have a loop of yarn—the stitch—sticking out of the bead.
- Replace the stitch onto the left hand needle. The bead is sitting below the knitting needle.
- (RS): Knit the stitch (or) (WS): Purl the stitch.

Instructions
Body
Picot hem:
With smaller needle, provisionally cast on 208 (240, 256, 288, 320, 336, 368) sts.
Join in the round, being careful not to twist. Pm for beginning of round.
Knit 9 rnds.
Picot rnd: *Yo, k2tog; rep from * to end.
Change to larger needle. Knit 9 rnds.
Hem rnd: Place sts from provisional CO onto the smaller needle. Fold hem with wrong sides together, smaller needle behind working needle. *K1 from front needle tog with 1 from back needle; rep from * to end.

Beaded border:
Knit 2 rnds.
Work the 15 rnds of Body Border chart.
Next rnd: K26 (30, 32, 36, 40, 42, 46) sts, pm for dart, k52 (60, 64, 72, 80, 84, 92) sts, pm for dart, k26 (30, 32, 36, 40, 42, 46) sts, pm for side. Repeat placement of shaping markers for back (total of six markers in work).

Waist shaping:
Dec 4 sts on next rnd, then every foll 3rd rnd 12 more times as foll: [Knit to 2 sts before dart marker, ssk, sm, knit to next dart marker, sm, k2tog] twice, knit to end. 156 (188, 204, 236, 268, 284, 316) sts
Work even for 2in / 5cm.
Inc 4 sts on next rnd, then every foll 4th rnd 9 more times as foll: [Knit to 1 st before dart marker, m1R, k1, sm, knit to next dart marker, sm, k1, m1L] twice, knit to end. 196 (228, 244, 276, 308, 324, 356) sts
Work even for ¼ (¼, ¼, ¼, ½, ½, ¾)in / 1.5 (1.5, 1.5, 1.5, 2, 2, 2.5)

cm, removing the four dart markers as you come to them.

Begin neckline chart:
Next rnd: K38 (46, 50, 58, 66, 70, 78)sts, pm for Neckline chart, work chart, pm, knit to end. 197 (229, 245, 277, 309, 325, 357) sts.
Continue in pattern, placing beads as charted, through Rnd 21 of the chart.
On Row 22, you will separate front from back, and begin working flat.
Work Row 22 of chart, then follow directions for right armhole bind off.
Work through Row 23 of chart, then follow directions for left armhole bindoff.
Work Row 24 to end of left front (stitch 9), turn, and continue working left front separate from right front.
After you complete the left front you will rejoin yarn at the right neckline edge and work the remainder of Row 24 for the right front.

Initial armhole bind off — separate front from back:
Rnd 22: BO 2 (2, 2, 2, 4, 5, 6) sts, work in pattern to side marker, turn.
Row 23 (WS): BO 2 (2, 2, 2, 4, 5, 6) sts, work in pattern to end of row. 47 (55, 59, 67, 73, 76, 83) sts each side of neck.

Left Front
Read ahead: armhole shaping, neck shaping, and beading are worked simultaneously.

Armhole shaping:
Bind off 3 sts at beg of next 0 (0, 0, 0, 0, 1, 1) RS rows (if number is 0, omit these rows).
Bind off 2 sts at beg of next 0 (0, 1, 2, 4, 3, 6) RS rows (if number is 0, omit these rows).
Dec 1 st at armhole edge on every RS row 5 (9, 9, 11, 9, 9, 6) times as foll: K1, ssk, work in patt to end. After armhole shaping is complete, begin slipping the first st of every RS row.

AT THE SAME TIME, continue to shape neck and place beads according to chart through Row 37. 7 sts dec'd at neck edge. After Row 37, continue to dec at neck edge as established on every RS row 19 (17, 15, 9, 9, 9, 9) times more, then on every other RS row 0 (2, 4, 10, 10, 10, 10) times, while placing beads as foll:

Row 1 (RS): Place Egg Shell bead such that it will be on the 3rd st from the neck edge after any subsequent decreases.
Row 2 (WS): P4, place Red bead, purl to end.
Row 3: Place Emerald bead such that it will be on the 6th st from the neck edge after any subsequent decs.
Row 4: No bead.
Row 5: Place Egg Shell bead such that it will be on the 3rd st from the neck edge after any subsequent decreases.
Row 6: P4, place Red bead, purl to end.
Rows 7-8: No bead.
Rep Rows 1-8.

After all shaping is complete, 16 (20, 22, 26, 30, 32, 36) sts rem.
Work even, slipping first st of each row and continuing to place beads as established, until armhole measures 6¼ (6¾, 7¼, 7¾, 8¼, 8½, 8¾)in / 16 (17, 18.5, 19.5, 21, 21.5, 22)cm, ending with a RS row.

Shoulder shaping:
Row 1 (WS): Sl1, work 12 (15, 16, 19, 22, 24, 27) sts, wrap next st, turn.
Row 2 (RS): Sl1, work in patt to end.
Row 3: Sl1, work 8 (10, 10, 12, 14, 16, 18) sts, wrap next st, turn.
Row 4: Sl1, work in patt to end.
Row 5: Sl1, work 4 (5, 5, 6, 7, 8, 9) sts, wrap next st, turn.
Row 6: Sl1, work in patt to end.
Row 7: Sl1, work in patt to end, concealing wraps.
Row 8: Sl1, work in patt to end.
Place sts on waste yarn or holder.

Right Front
Read ahead; armhole shaping, neck shaping, and beading are worked simultaneously.

Join yarn at neck edge. Work in patt (chart Row 24) to end.

Armhole shaping:
Bind off 3 sts at beg of next 0 (0, 0, 0, 0, 1, 1) WS rows (if number is 0, omit these rows).
Bind off 2 sts at beg of next 0 (0, 1, 2, 4, 3, 6) WS rows (if number is 0, omit these rows).
Dec 1 st at armhole edge on every RS row 5 (9, 9, 11, 9, 9, 6) times as foll: Work in patt to last 3 sts, k2tog, k1. After armhole shaping is complete, begin slipping the first st of every WS row.

AT THE SAME TIME, continue to shape neck and place beads according to chart through Row 37. 7 sts dec'd at neck edge. After Row 37, continue to dec at neck edge as established on every RS row 19 (17, 15, 9, 9, 9, 9) times more, then on every other RS row 0 (2, 4, 10, 10, 10, 10) times, while placing beads as foll:

Row 1 (RS): Place Egg Shell bead such that it is on the 3rd st from the neck edge after any decreases.
Row 2 (WS): Work to 5 sts from end, place Red bead, p4.
Row 3: Place Emerald bead such that it is on the 6th st from the neck edge after any decreases.
Row 4: No bead.
Row 5: Place Egg Shell bead such that it is on the 3rd st from the neck edge after any decreases.
Row 6: Work to 5 sts from end, place Red bead, p4.
Row 7: No bead.
Row 8: No bead.
Rep Rows 1-8.

After all shaping is complete, 16 (20, 22, 26, 30, 32, 36) sts rem.
Work even, slipping the first st of every row and continuing to place beads as established, until armhole measures 6¼ (6¾, 7¼, 7¾, 8¼, 8½, 8¾)in / 16 (17, 18.5, 19.5, 21, 21.5, 22)cm, ending with a WS row.

Shoulder shaping:
Row 1 (RS): Sl1, work 12 (15, 16, 19, 22, 24, 27) sts, wrap next st, turn.
Row 2 (WS): Sl1, work in patt to end.
Row 3: Sl1, work 8 (10, 10, 12, 14, 16, 18) sts, wrap next st, turn.
Row 4: Sl1, work in patt to end.
Row 5: Sl1, work 4 (5, 5, 6, 7, 8, 9) sts, wrap next st, turn.

Row 6: Sl1, work in patt to end.
Row 7: Sl1, work in patt to end, concealing wraps.
Place sts on waste yarn or holder.

Back
Join yarn at right underarm with RS facing.
BO 2 (2, 2, 2, 4, 5, 6) sts at beg of next 2 rows. 94 (110, 118, 134, 146, 152, 166) sts.
BO 3 sts at beg of next 0 (0, 0, 0, 0, 2, 2) rows (if number is 0, omit these rows).
BO 2 sts at beg of next 0 (0, 2, 4, 8, 6, 12) rows (if number is 0, omit these rows).
94 (110, 114, 126, 130, 134, 136) sts.
Dec 1 st at each armhole on every RS row 5 (9, 9, 11, 9, 9, 6) times as foll: K1, ssk, work to 3 sts before end, k2tog, k1. 84 (92, 96, 104, 112, 116, 124) sts.
Work even, slipping the first stitch of every row, until armholes measure 5¼ (5¾, 6¼, 6¾, 7¼, 7½, 7¾)in / 13.5 (14.5, 16, 17, 18.5, 19.5, 21)cm, ending with a RS row.

Neckline beading:
Next row (WS): Sl1, p13 (17, 19, 23, 27, 29, 33), pm for chart, p28, m1p, p28, pm for chart, purl to end. 85 (93, 97, 105, 113, 117, 125) sts.
Next row (RS): Work even, working Back Neck chart between markers.
Work through Row 6 of chart.
Next row (RS): Work 20 (24, 26, 30, 34, 36, 40) sts, BO center 45 sts, work to end.

Left neck and shoulder shaping:
Row 1 (WS) (Row 8 of chart): Work even in pattern.
Row 2 (RS) (Row 9 of chart): BO 4 sts, work in patt to end. 16 (20, 22, 26, 30, 32, 36) sts.
Row 3: Work even in patt.
Row 4: Sl1, work 12 (15, 16, 19, 22, 24, 27) sts, wrap next st, turn.
Row 5: Sl1, work in patt to end.
Row 6: Sl1, work 8 (10, 10, 12, 14, 16, 18) sts, wrap next st, turn.
Row 7: Sl1, work in patt to end.
Row 8: Sl1, work 4 (5, 5, 6, 7, 8, 9) sts, wrap next st, turn.
Row 9: Sl1, work in patt to end.
Row 10: Sl1, work in patt to end, concealing wraps.
Place sts on waste yarn or holder.

Right neck and shoulder shaping:
Join yarn at neck edge with WS facing.
Row 1 (WS) (Row 8 of chart): BO 4 sts, work in patt to end. 16 (20, 22, 26, 30, 32, 36) sts.
Row 2 (RS) (Row 9 of chart): Sl1, work in patt to end.
Row 3: Sl1, work 12 (15, 16, 19, 22, 24, 27) sts, wrap next st, turn.
Row 4: Sl1, work in patt to end.
Row 5: Sl1, work 8 (10, 10, 12, 14, 16, 18) sts, wrap next st, turn.
Row 6: Sl1, work in patt to end.
Row 7: Sl1, work 4 (5, 5, 6, 7, 8, 9) sts, wrap next st, turn.
Row 8: Sl1, work in patt to end.
Row 9: Sl1, work in patt to end, concealing wraps.
Row 10: Sl1, work in patt to end.

Join Fronts to Back
Using a 3-needle BO, join the shoulders.

Sleeves
Starting at center underarm and working clockwise around armhole, pick up (do not knit, just pick up) 68 (74, 80, 92, 100, 104, 114) sts. Pm for beginning of round at center underarm.
Work short rows to shape sleeve cap as described below, but do NOT conceal wraps. (Leaving the wraps covers any gaps you may have from picking up the stitches; the wraps actually look like legs of the stitch below.)
Short Row 1 (RS): Join yarn beginning at stitch 23 (25, 27, 31, 34, 35, 39); knit to stitch 46 (50, 54, 62, 67, 70, 76), wrap next st, turn.
Short Row 2 (WS): Purl back to and including first stitch worked, wrap next st, turn.
Short Rows 3 & 4: Work in pattern to wrapped st, work wrapped st, wrap next st, turn.
Repeat Short Row 3 and Row 4 until 4 (6, 7, 7, 8, 8, 11) unworked sts rem between last wrapped st and marker, ending with a WS row. Turn and begin working in the round. Work even until sleeve measures 8¼ (8¾, 8¼, 9½, 10¼, 9¼, 9¾)in / 21 (22, 21, 24, 26, 23.5, 24.5)cm from shoulder. On last rnd, pm for center of sleeve as foll: K34 (37, 40, 46, 50, 52, 57), pm, knit to end.

Sleeve shaping:
Dec 1 st at each end of next rnd, then every foll 10th (8th, 8th, 6th, 5th, 6th, 5th) rnd 13 (16, 17, 21, 25, 23, 28) more times as foll: K1, k2tog, work to 3 sts before end, ssk, k1. 40 (40, 44, 48, 48, 56, 56) sts.

AT THE SAME TIME, when sleeve measures 17¾ (18¼, 18½, 18¾, 19½, 19¾, 20½)in / 45(46.5, 47, 47.5, 49.5, 50.5, 52)cm from shoulder, begin working sleeve beading: Work in pattern to 20 (20, 20, 24, 24, 28, 28) sts before center marker. Pm for beginning of chart, work first row of Sleeve Border chart over 41 (41, 41, 49, 49, 57, 57) sts removing center marker as you go, pm for end of chart, work in pattern to end.
Continue as established (working sleeve decreases until completed then working even) until last rnd of chart is completed. Note the sleeve decreases are not shown on the chart.

Picot hem:
Knit 11 rnds even.
Picot rnd: *Yo, k2tog; rep from * to end.
Change to smaller needles. Knit 9 rnds.
Cut yarn, leaving a tail 3 times the circumference of the cuff. Fold hem with wrong sides facing and sew live sts to corresponding purl bump using the yarn tail.

Finishing
Beginning at left shoulder seam, with RS facing and smaller needles pick up and knit 120 (125, 135, 140, 145, 150, 150) sts around neckline. Pm for beg of rnd. Knit 4 rnds. BO.

Weave in ends. Block.

Tiles schematic

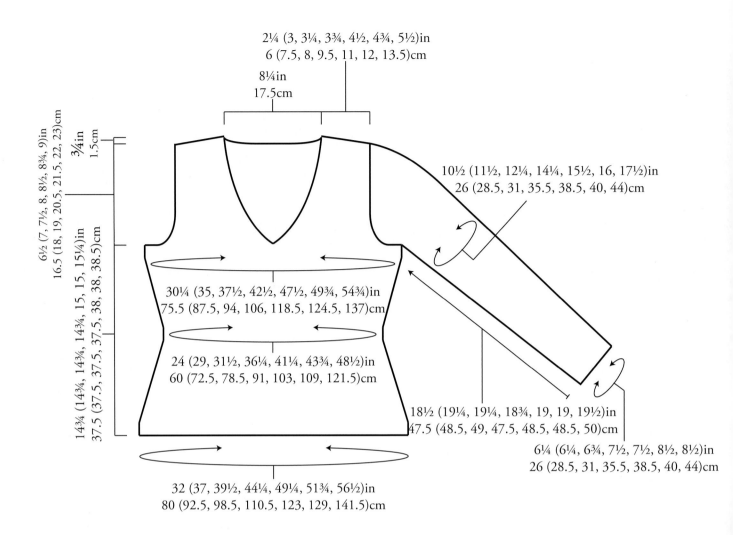

2¼ (3, 3¼, 3¾, 4½, 4¾, 5½)in
6 (7.5, 8, 9.5, 11, 12, 13.5)cm

8¼in
17.5cm

¾in
1.5cm

6½ (7, 7½, 8, 8½, 8¾, 9)in
16.5 (18, 19, 20.5, 21.5, 22, 23)cm

14¾ (14¾, 14¾, 14¾, 15, 15, 15¼)in
37.5 (37.5, 37.5, 37.5, 38, 38, 38.5)cm

10½ (11½, 12¼, 14¼, 15½, 16, 17½)in
26 (28.5, 31, 35.5, 38.5, 40, 44)cm

30¼ (35, 37½, 42½, 47½, 49¾, 54¾)in
75.5 (87.5, 94, 106, 118.5, 124.5, 137)cm

24 (29, 31½, 36¼, 41¼, 43¾, 48½)in
60 (72.5, 78.5, 91, 103, 109, 121.5)cm

18½ (19¼, 19¼, 18¾, 19, 19, 19½)in
47.5 (48.5, 49, 47.5, 48.5, 48.5, 50)cm

6¼ (6¼, 6¾, 7½, 7½, 8½, 8½)in
26 (28.5, 31, 35.5, 38.5, 40, 44)cm

32 (37, 39½, 44¼, 49¼, 51¾, 56½)in
80 (92.5, 98.5, 110.5, 123, 129, 141.5)cm

Body border chart

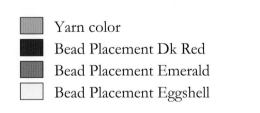

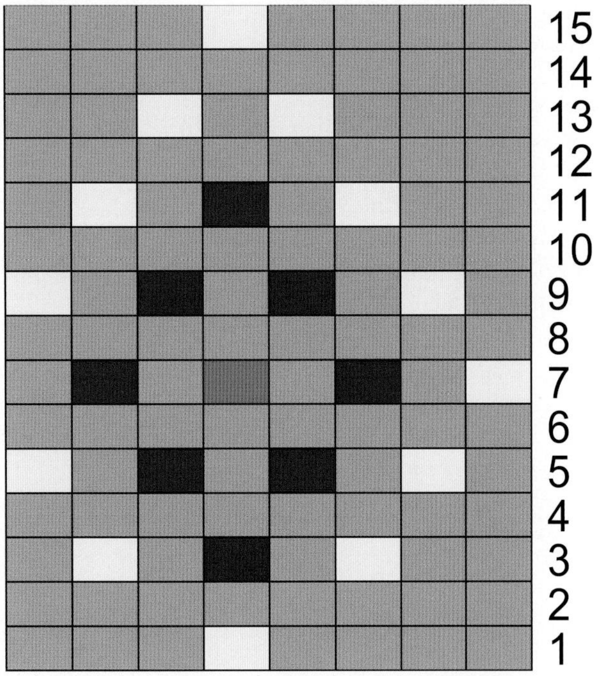

15
14
13
12
11
10
9
8
7
6
5
4
3
2
1

Legend

Yarn color

Bead Placement Dk Red

Bead Placement Emerald

Bead Placement Eggshell

 bo

 ssk

 k2tog

mr m1r

k

FRONT NECKLINE CHART

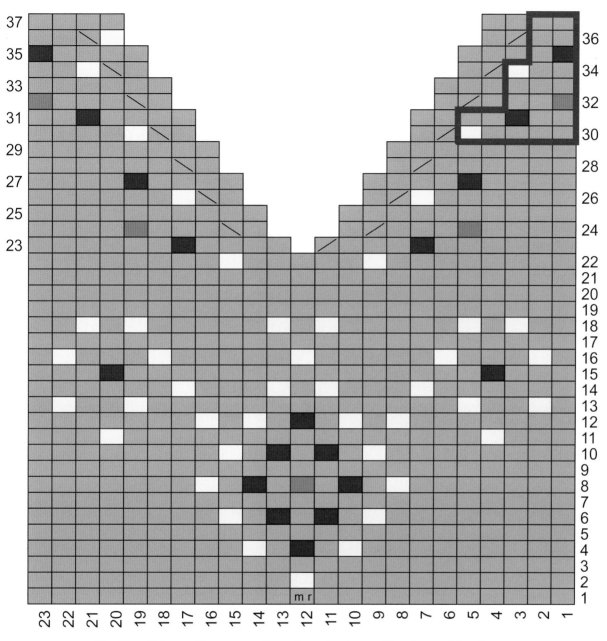

On Row 22, you'll separate front from back, and begin working flat.
Work Row 22 of chart, then follow directions for right armhole bind off.
Work through Row 23 of chart, then follow directions for left armhole bindoff.
Work Row 24 to end of left front (stitch 9), turn, and continue working left front separate from right front.
After you complete the left front you'll rejoin yarn at the right neckline edge and work the remainder of Row 24 for the right front.

BACK NECKLINE CHART

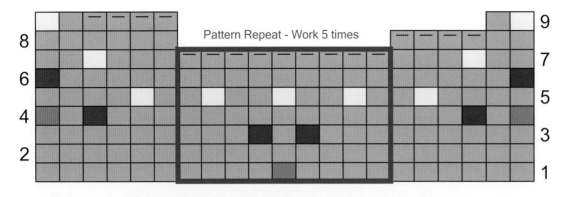

Pattern Repeat - Work 5 times

Sleeve border chart for XS, S, M, 2X, 3x

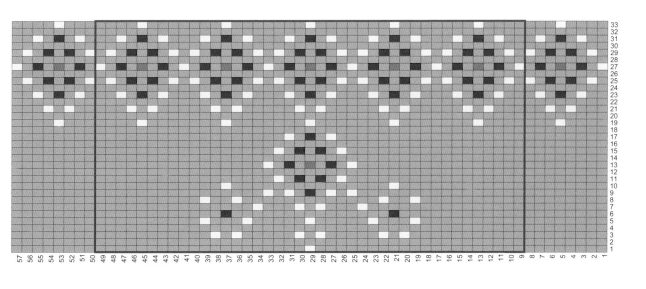

━━ Size XS, S, M between borders

Sleeve border chart for L, XL

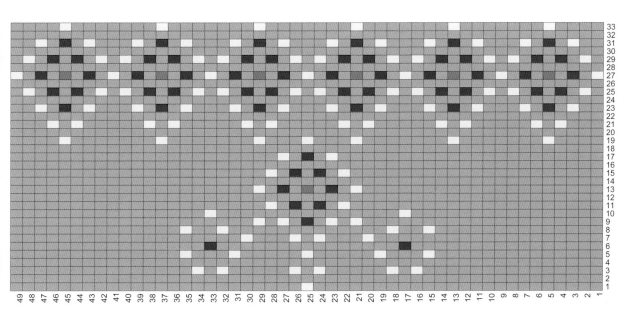

Peacock Shawl

I wanted to design a shawl that incorporated traditional lace patterns, reminiscent of peacock feathers, into a simple rectangular shawl. This is a good first lace piece for a confident knitter, but still has enough going on to maintain your interest if you've more experience.

The shawl is very easy to resize; since all the repeats across the different stitch patterns are the same width, simply work more (or fewer) panels. Of course length is also easily changed by working more or fewer repeats of each stitch pattern.

Worked in luxurious Blue Sky Alpacas Alpaca Silk, the Peacock Shawl would make a treasured gift—if you can bear to remove it from your own shoulders!

Size: One

Finished Measurements
Approx. 18in / 45.5cm by 66in / 167.5cm, blocked.

Yarn
Blue Sky Alpacas Alpaca Silk, 50% alpaca/50% silk, 146 yds / 50g, 5 skeins in Blueberry

Needles
US 5 (3.75mm) needles

Gauge
Approx. 15 sts and 24 rows = 4in / 10cm in Section A lace pattern, blocked. Gauge is not critical, but alterations to gauge can affect yarn requirements.

Notions & Other Supplies
Yarn needle, waste yarn
Stitch markers as desired

Required Skills
Simple lace, grafting

Pattern Notes
Only RS rows are shown on charts. Work WS rows as directed in text.
Shawl is knitted in two halves that are then grafted together.

Instructions
Loosely cast on 77 sts.
Row 1 (WS): P2, k1, p71, k1, p2.
Row 2 (RS): Work RS rows as charted. Stitches bordered in red are pattern repeats. Work sts 1-14, repeat sts 15-24 five times, work sts 25-37.
Row 3 and all WS rows through Row 11 of Section C: Sl1 wyif, p1, k1, p71, k1, p2.

Odd rows from Row 13 of Section C to end: Sl1 wyif, p1, k2, *p9, k1; rep from * to 3 sts before end, k1, p2.
Work Section A, Rows 1-26 once; Section B, Rows 1-28 twice; Section C, Rows 1-14 once; Section D, Rows 1-8 five times; and Section E, Rows 1-4 sixteen times.
Put sts on waste yarn.

Repeat for second half.
Graft together. Block.

Chart Key
☐ RS: k; WS: p
● RS: p; WS: k
☑ RS: k2tog; WS: p2tog
◯ RS & WS: yo
☒ RS: s1-k2tog-psso; WS: sssp
☐ RS: ssk; WS: ssp
☑ RS: s1; WS: s1 wyif

Section E

Work 16 times.

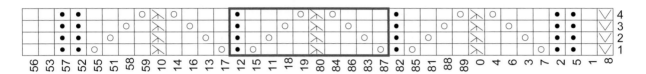

Section D

Work 5 times.

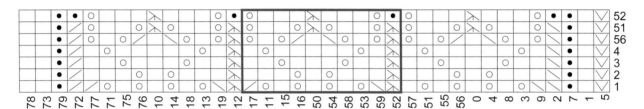

Section C

Work once.

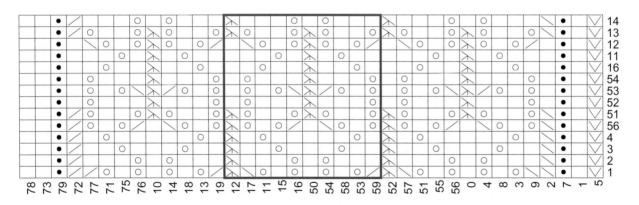

Section B

Work twice.

Section A

Work once.

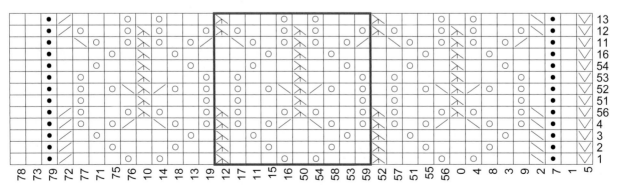

Stitches bordered in red are pattern repeats. Work sts 1-14, repeat sts 15-24 to 12 sts before end, work sts 25-37.

UnderSea Garden Cowl

The main stitch pattern in this quick-to-knit cowl is a variation of Print O' the Wave. To me it looks like kelp, which grows in abundance along the California coast, including around Catalina. It's also incorporated in the Undersea Garden tiled mural at the Avalon Casino.

The fingering weight version, shown in Bijou Basin Lhasa Wilderness, is wonderfully soft and drapey. The lace weight version, shown in Knit Picks Aloft, is airy and delicate.

Sizes
Laceweight (fingering weight)

Finished Measurements
Approx. 11 (10)in / 28 (25.5)cm tall by 17¼in / 44cm circumference

Yarn
Laceweight: Knit Picks Aloft, 75% super kid mohair/25% silk, 246 yds / 25g, 1 ball in Tranquility
Fingering weight: Bijou Bijou Spun Lhasa Wilderness, 75% yak/25% bamboo, 180 yds / 56g, 1 skein in Sky

Needles
US 3 (3.25mm) 16in / 40cm circular, or size to obtain gauge.

Gauge
26 sts and 38 rnds = 4in / 10cm in center lace pattern (chart Rows 20-31 or 24-35), blocked. Gauge is not critical; swatch to determine your desired fabric. However, keep in mind that alterations to gauge can affect yarn requirements; knit to gauge, the fingering weight version takes just under 1 skein. Purchase an additional skein if you'd like a looser gauge.

Notions & Other Supplies
Beads Size 6/0 (laceweight version only): 112 if knit as shown. 16 total beads for edging, 96 beads for center
.8mm steel crochet hook for beading (laceweight version only)
Yarn needle
Minimum one stitch marker for beginning of round, others as desired to mark pattern repeats

HOW TO PLACE BEADS:

* Work up to the stitch that will have a bead.
* Place the bead onto the crochet hook.
* Grab the stitch on the left hand needle with the hook. I pull tightly so that the yarn is as snug as possible against the crochet hook.
* Pull the bead over the yarn. You should have a loop of yarn—the stitch—sticking out of the bead.
* Replace the stitch onto the left hand needle. The bead is sitting below the knitting needle.
* Knit the stitch.

Instructions
CO 112 sts using a stretchy cast on, such as the backwards loop (shown) or long-tail methods. Join in the round, being careful not to twist, and PM for beginning of round.

Note:
If you prefer, for the laceweight version, cast on 113 sts, work the first 3 rows of the chart flat up to the last stitch of the third row, then join in the round by purling the first stitch of the fourth row and last stitch of the third row together. This may be easier, especially with a slippery laceweight, than trying to immediately join in the round.

Work the bottom edging (Rows 1-19 [1-23]).
Begin working center lace pattern (Rows 20-31 [24-35]).
Work a total of 6 (5) repeats of the center pattern (72 [60] rows).
Begin working top edging (Rows 32-49 [36-57]).
BO loosely.

I used Jeny's Surprisingly Stretchy Bind Off; http://knitty.com/ISSUEfall09/FEATjssbo.php. Weave in loose ends. Block. The center portion naturally biases to the right, but you can block it straight if desired. Block points in the top to mirror the bottom points formed by the edging stitch pattern.

Laceweight chart

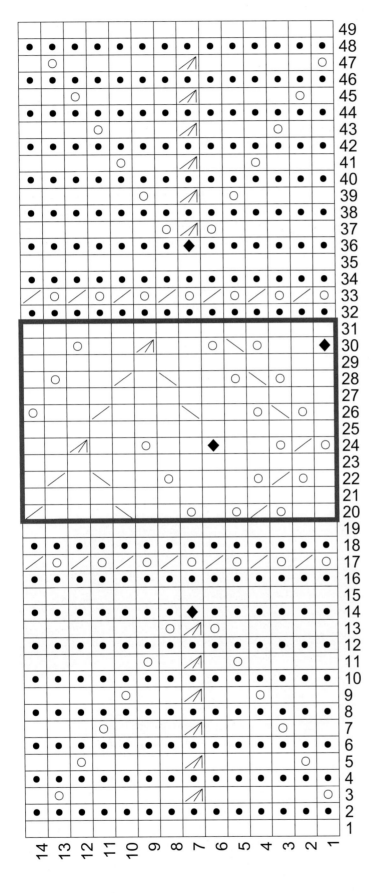

Fingering weight chart

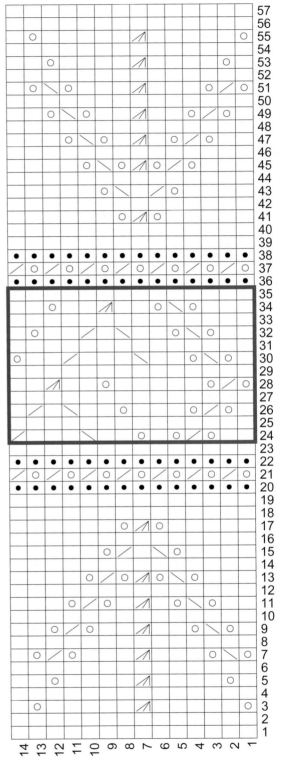

	k
○	yo
⟋⟋	k3tog
⟋	k2tog
⟍	ssk
•	p

Laceweight (above) and fingering weight (below) versions of the cowl.

STAIR STEPS TAM

> *Stair risers are a popular place for tiles! Often the home builder used different tiles for each step, as I used different motifs.*

Size
One size, to fit head circumference 21-23in / 53.5-58.5cm

Finished Measurements
Brim circumference 18in / 45.5cm

Yarn
Hazel Knits Artisan Sock, 90% merino wool/10% nylon, 400 yds / 120g, 1 skein in Equinox (MC) and 25g (approx. ¼ skein) each in Rick's Cognac, Hoppy Blonde, Saffron, Beachglass, Aquarius, and Lime Granita.

Needles
US 2½ (3mm) circular(s) or double pointed as preferred, or size to obtain gauge.
US 2 (2.75mm) for ribbing, or one size smaller than for body of tam.

Gauge
32 sts and 36 rnds = 4in / 10cm in stranded stockinette stitch with larger needles.

Notions & Other Supplies
Yarn needle, 8 stitch markers (one unique for beginning of round).

Required Skills
Knitting in the round, stranded knitting, chart reading.

Pattern Notes
For the sk2p decreases, slip the last stitch of the round preceding the decrease round and use this stitch as the slipped stitch for the first sk2p of the decrease round. (Slip the last stitch of the round to the right hand needle, remove stitch marker, slip stitch back to left hand needle, place marker on right hand needle (new beginning of round).)

Instructions
Brim
CO 144 sts in MC using smaller needles. Join in the round, being careful not to twist. PM for beginning of round.
Work corrugated ribbing as charted (Rnds 1-10).

Body of Tam
Change to larger needles. Work Rnds 11-85 (8 repeats of chart per round), placing markers between repeats if desired. See pattern notes regarding sk2p prior to working Rnd 51 and other decrease rounds. At completion of chart, 8 sts rem.
Break yarn leaving a tail, draw through rem sts and fasten off.

Finishing
Weave in any loose ends. Block over a dinner plate.

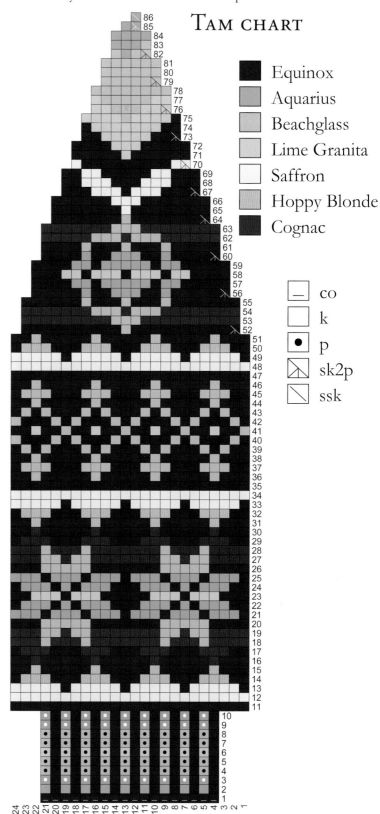

TAM CHART

◼	Equinox
◼	Aquarius
◼	Beachglass
◼	Lime Granita
◻	Saffron
◼	Hoppy Blonde
◼	Cognac

—	co
□	k
•	p
⧅	sk2p
◹	ssk

45

Stair Steps Fingerless Mitts

> *Just 100g of Equinox and 25g each of other colors is enough for mitts **and** tam!*

Size
S/M (M/L)

Finished measurements
Hand circumference 8 (9)in / 20.5 (23)cm

Yarn
Hazel Knits Artisan Sock, 90% merino wool/10% nylon, 400 yds /120g, 1 skein in Equinox (MC) and 25g (approx. ¼ skein) each in Rick's Cognac, Hoppy Blonde, Saffron, Beachglass, Aquarius, and Lime Granita.

Needles
US 2½ (3mm) circular(s) or double pointed as preferred, or size to obtain gauge.

Gauge
32 sts and 36 rnds = 4in / 10cm in stranded stockinette stitch

Notions & Other Supplies
Yarn needle, 3 stitch markers (one unique for beginning of round), waste yarn.

Required Skills
Knitting in the round, stranded knitting, chart reading.

Cuff
With MC, CO 54 (60) stitches using the long tail cast on with tail end of yarn held doubled. PM for beginning of round.
Rnd 1: *[K1 tbl] twice, p1; rep from * to end.
Rep Rnd 1 until cuff measures 1½in / 4cm or desired length.

Palm
Size S/M only: *K9, m1; rep from * to end. 60 sts.
Size M/L only: *K1, [m1, k7] 4 times, k1; rep from * once. 68 sts.
Work Right or Left chart in your size. Place markers for thumb gusset as noted on chart. Rnd 36 place the thumb sts on waste yarn, CO 4 st using the backward loop cast on method in indicated colors, and continue working the rest of the chart. 63 (72) sts at completion of chart.

Upper Cuff
After completing the chart, knit 1 rnd in MC.
Work in twisted 2x1 ribbing as for Cuff for 1in / 2.5cm or desired length.
BO in pattern.

Thumb
Replace the 27 held sts onto your needles. Working with MC, pick up and knit 2 sts in the gap, work to end of round in MC, then pick up and knit 2 additional sts in the gap.
31 sts.
Next rnd: Knit to 1 st before end of round. Knit this st tog with first stitch of round. 30 sts.
Knit 1 rnd.
Work in twisted 2x1 ribbing as for Cuff for ½in / 1.5cm or desired length.
BO in pattern.

Finishing
Weave in any loose ends.

S/M Left Mitt

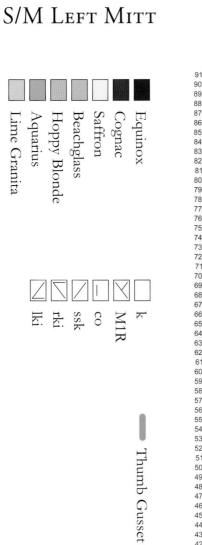

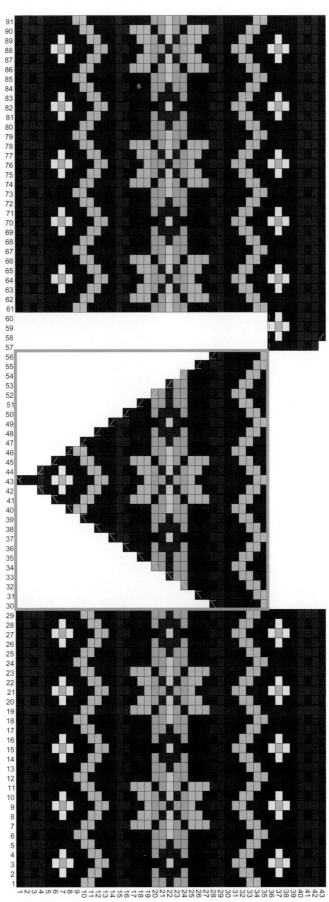

S/M Right Mitt

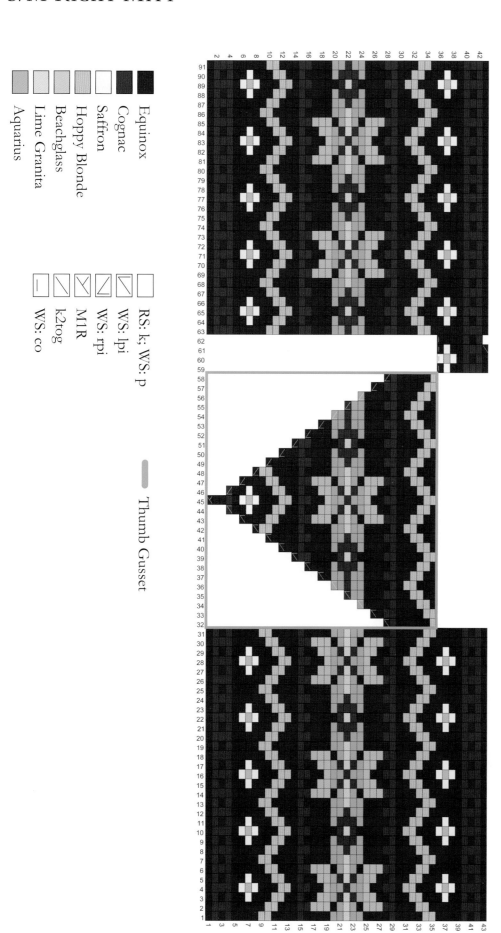

Equinox
Cognac
Saffron
Hoppy Blonde
Beachglass
Lime Granita
Aquarius

RS: k; WS: p
WS: lpi
WS: rpi
M1R
k2tog
WS: co

Thumb Gusset

M/L Left Mitt

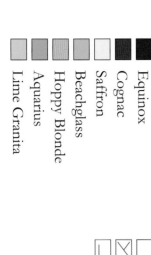

Lime Granita
Aquarius
Hoppy Blonde
Beachglass
Saffron
Cognac
Equinox

— co
⊠ M1R
☐ k

━ Thumb Gusset

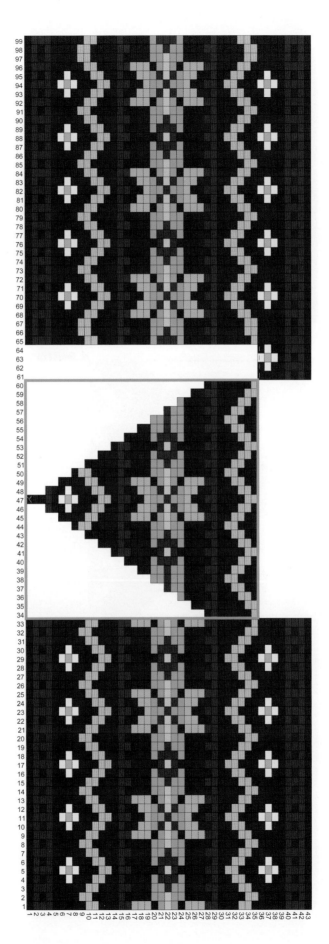

M/L Right Mitt

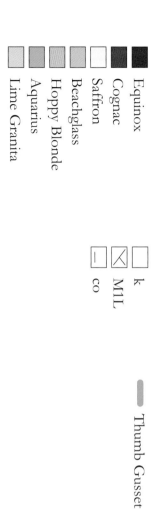

Lime Granita
Aquarius
Hoppy Blonde
Beachglass
Saffron
Cognac
Equinox

k
M1L
co

Thumb Gusset

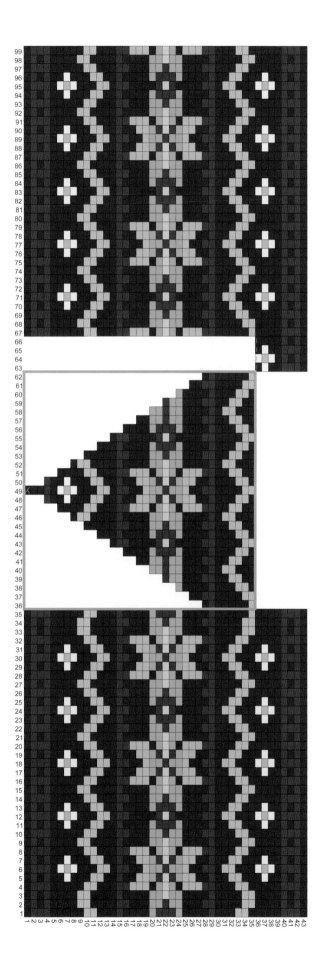

FRINGE SOCKS

Adamson House has two iconic pieces of tilework. The first is the peacock fountain; the second is the tiled fringed Persian rug.

This 'rug' is reason alone to visit the Adamson House. Featuring dozens of colors, it dominates the hallway in which it was installed. It's a triumph of trompe l'oeil—the detail is amazing, including the fringe which waves and overlaps like real fringe.

I love the fringe, which is why it's what I wanted to reinterpret in a knitted piece. My intent was to evoke the edge of a Persian carpet including the fringe.

Size
S (M, L)

Finished Measurements
7½ (8¼, 9)in / 19 (21, 23)cm foot circumference.

Yarn
Little Red Bicycle Tandem Sock, 80% wool/20% nylon, 400 yds / 100g, 1 skein each Vixen (MC) and Basque (CC)

Needles
US size 1 (2.25mm) circular(s) or double pointed as preferred, or size to obtain gauge.

Gauge
34 sts & 40 rounds = 4in /10cm in stranded stockinette stitch
32 sts & 40 rounds = 4in / 10cm in stockinette stitch

Notions & Other Supplies
Yarn needle, stitch markers, cable needle if you use one.

Skills Required
Stranded knitting, working in the round, picking up stitches, Kitchener stitch, braids

Pattern Notes
A full braid consists of 2 rounds. The first charted row of the braid corresponds to the first round as described; the second charted row corresponds to the second round. See page 56 for braid directions.

Cuff and Leg
Cast on 66 (72, 78) sts. Join for working in the round, being careful not to twist. PM for beginning of round. Work the chart for your size. 60 (66, 72) sts rem at end.
Continue in MC in stockinette stitch until leg is 7.5"/ 17.5 cm long (or desired length).

Heel Flap
Work heel flap flat as follows over 30 (32, 36) sts.

Row 1 (WS): Sl1, purl to end.
Row 2 (RS): *Sl1, k1; rep from * to end.
Rep these two rows 15 (16, 17) times more, then the WS row once more. Total of 33 (35, 37) rows.

Turn Heel
Row 1 (RS): Sl1, k16 (18, 20), ssk, k1, turn.
Row 2: Sl1, p5 (7, 9), p2tog, p1, turn.
Row 3: Sl1, knit until 1 st before the gap, ssk, k1, turn.
Row 4: Sl1, purl until 1 st before the gap, p2tog, p1, turn.
Rep Rows 3 and 4 until all sts at either end are used up. 18 (20, 22) sts.

Gusset
K9 (10, 11) sts, pm for new beg of rnd, k9 (10, 11) sts, pick up and knit 16 (17, 18) sts along edge of flap, pm for instep, work 30 (34, 36) instep sts, pm for instep, pick up and knit 16 (17, 18) sts along edge of flap, knit to end of rnd. 80 (88, 94) sts.
Work 1 rnd even.
Dec rnd: Knit to 2 sts before instep marker, k2tog, sm, knit across instep, sm, ssk, work to end of rnd.
Rep these two rnds until 60 (66, 72) sts rem.

Foot
Work in St st to 2in / 5cm less than desired finished length. For size M only, shift one of the instep markers over by 1 st, so that sole and instep each have 33 sts.

Toe
Rnd 1: Knit to last 2 sole sts, k2tog, ssk, knit to last 2 instep sts, k2tog, ssk, knit to end.
Rnd 2: Knit.
Rep these two rnds until 20 (26, 32) sts remain. Knit to end of sole sts. Use Kitchener stitch to graft the toe sts together.

Finishing
Weave in loose ends. Block.

Size small chart

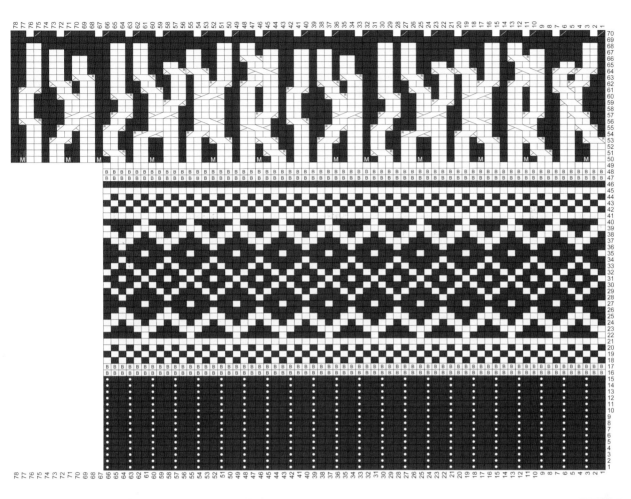

Size large chart

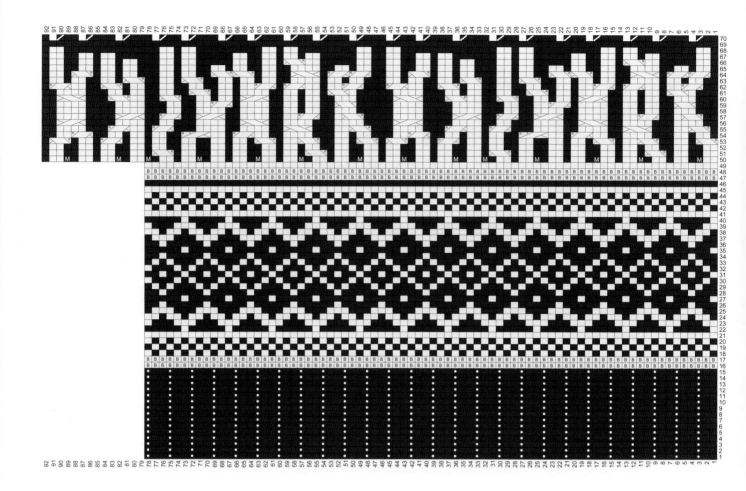

2/1 LC
Slip 2 stitches to cable needle and hold in front; k1; k2 from cable needle.

2/1 LC red background
Slip 2 sts to cable needle and hold in front; k1 in MC. K2 from cable needle with CC.

2/1 RC red background
Slip 1 stitch to cable needle and hold in back; k2 with CC; k1 from cable needle with MC.

2/2 LC
Slip 2 stitches to cable needle and hold in front; k2; k2 from cable needle.

2/2 RC
Slip 2 stitches to cable needle and hold in back; k2; k2 from cable needle.

2/2 RC with red background
Slip 2 sts to cable needle and hold in back; k2 with CC; k2 from cable needle with MC.

Braids

Work braids as follows:

Rnd 1: Hold both strands of yarn in front as if to purl. P1 with MC, bringing yarn over MC strand. P1 with CC, bringing yarn over MC strand. Repeat to end of round.

Rnd 2: Hold both strands of yarn in front. P1 with MC, bringing yarn under MC strand. P1 with CC, bringing yarn under MC strand. Repeat to end of round.

Rnd 1 will twist the yarn; Rnd 2 will untwist it, so resist untwisting as you go!

Note that the braid for this pattern doesn't require a MC, CC set up row; the center purl bumps are all in MC.

You can choose to work Rnd 2 first, then Rnd 1; this changes the "direction" of the braid points.

FRINGE SOCKS LEGEND

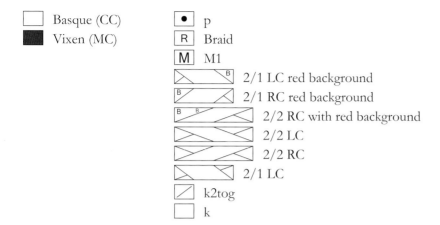

☐ Basque (CC)

■ Vixen (MC)

•	p
R	Braid
M	M1

2/1 LC red background

2/1 RC red background

2/2 RC with red background

2/2 LC

2/2 RC

2/1 LC

k2tog

k

This tile "carpet" from the Adamson House (see page 10) inspired these Fringe Socks.

CATALINA STAR PILLOW

> The star, or compass face, was a common tile motif. Here it is interpreted as an intarsia motif.
>
> I wanted to make the back decorative, too, incorporating a geometric edging on the button bands. Feel free to use it as the front as well!

Size:
One size

Finished Measurements:
Approx 19in / 48.5cm square

Yarn
Black Water Abbey 2 Ply Worsted Weight, 100% Irish wool, 220 yds / 113g, in the following amounts and colorways:
MC Wheat, 3 oz
CC1 Chestnut, 6 oz
CC2 Wine, 1 oz
CC3 Grey Sea, 2 oz

Needles
US size 5 (3.75mm) or size to obtain gauge

Gauge
20 sts and 29 rows = 4in / 10cm in stockinette stitch

Notions & Other Supplies
Crochet hook to join pieces
Yarn needle
20"pillow form
4 1¼" buttons
Stitch markers as desired

Skills Required
Intarsia, single crochet for edging

Pattern Notes
Slip the first stitch of each row unless otherwise indicated.
Slip markers as you come to them unless otherwise indicated.

Stitches
Seed Stitch (multiple of 2 sts)
*K1, p1; rep from * to end.

Instructions
Front
With MC, cast on 96 sts.
Row 1 (WS): P1, work seed stitch to 1 st before end, p1.
Row 2 (RS): Sl1, work seed st to 1 st before end, k1.
Row 3: Sl1, work seed stitch to 1 st before end, p1.
Row 4: Sl1, 2 sts in seed stitch, work Front Chart over 90 sts, 2 sts in seed stitch, k1.

Row 5: Sl1, 2 sts in seed stitch, work Front Chart over 90 sts, 2 sts in seed stitch, p1.
Continue as established until all 136 rows of chart are complete.
Rep Rows 2-3.
Bind off.

Left Back
With CC1, cast on 64 sts.
Row 1 (WS): P1, work seed stitch to 1 st before end, p1.
Row 2 (RS): Sl1, work seed st to 1 st before end, k1.
Row 3: Sl1, work seed stitch to 1 st before end, p1.
Row 4: Work Left Border Chart over 19 sts, pm, knit to 3 sts before end, 2 sts in seed st, k1.
Row 5: Sl1, 2 sts in seed st, purl to m, work Left Border Chart.
Continue as established until all 136 rows of chart are complete.
Rep Rows 2-3.
Bind off.

Right Back
With CC1, cast on 42 sts.
Row 1 (WS): P1, work seed stitch to 1 st before end, p1.
Row 2 (RS): Sl1, work seed st to 1 st before end, k1.
Row 3: Sl1, work seed stitch to 1 st before end, p1.
Row 4: Sl1, 2 sts seed st, k20, pm, work Right Border Chart over 19 sts.
Row 5: Work Right Border Chart, purl to 3 sts before end, 2 sts seed st, p1.
Continue as established until all 136 rows of chart are complete.
Rep Rows 2-3.
Bind off.

Finishing
Weave in all ends. Block.
Sew buttons on Left Back.
Join pieces as follows: Pin all pieces together, buttoning left & right backs. Using CC1, single crochet all edges together, working through all three layers where back pieces overlap.

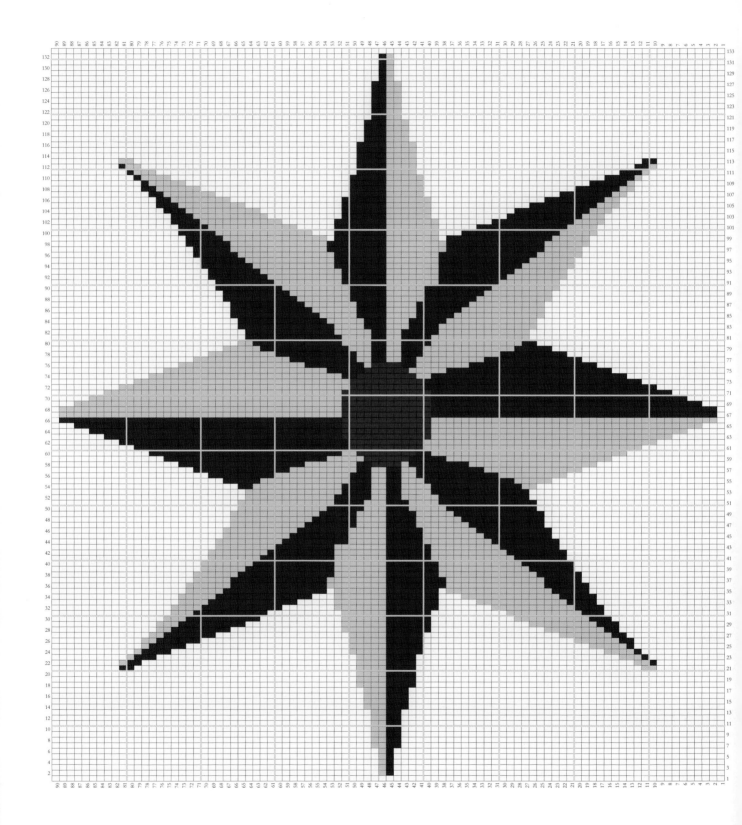

LEFT BACK CHART

RIGHT BACK CHART

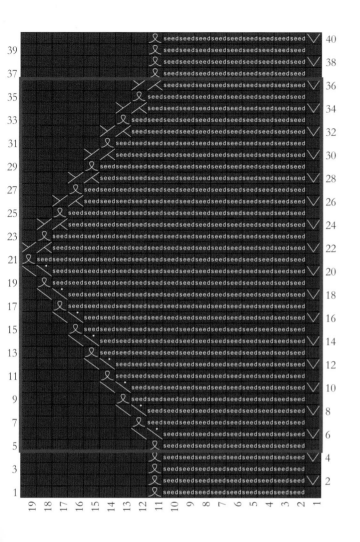

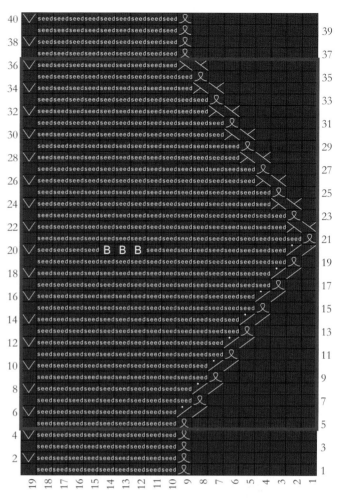

■	Wine	
■	Chestnut	
□	Wheat	
▨	Grey Sea	

□	RS: k; WS: p
℗	RS: k-tbl; WS: p-tbl
seed	RS & WS: Seed Stitch
⋁	s1
⟋	1/1 LPC
⟍	1/1 RC
⟋	1/1 RPC
B	Buttonhole
⟍	1/1 LC

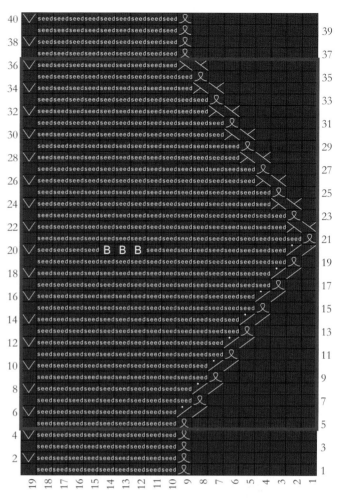

Wrought Cardi

Wrought iron gates, windows, screens, and stair railings can be incredibly detailed in examples of California Revival architecture. I wanted to play with the ways ironwork scrolls and twists across vertical ribs in these pieces. Twisted and twisted travelling stitches were the perfect way to translate this to knitting.

The trick with the cardi was to keep the feel of the other patterns without making it too complicated. One motif does have wrong side crosses, but they are simple and repetitive. All the other crosses occur on the right side until the very bottom of the cardi.

Size
XS (S, M, L, XL, 2X, 3X)

Finished Measurements
Chest (buttoned): 30¾ (34¾, 39¾, 42¾, 47¼, 51¼, 55¼)in / 77.5 (87, 99.5, 107, 118.5, 128, 138.5)cm

Yarn
Dragonfly Fibers Blue Face Worsted, 100% Bluefaced Leicester wool, 200 yds / 113g, 6 (7, 8, 8, 9, 10, 11) skeins in Dragonberry

Needles
US 6 (4mm) needles: long circular for body, circular(s) or double pointed for sleeves, or size to obtain gauge.

Gauge
19 sts and 28 rows = 4in / 10cm in stockinette stitch; 29 sts = 4in /10cm over twisted stitch panels.

Notions & Other Supplies
Yarn needle, waste yarn, minimum 2 stitch markers (others as desired), 4 1in / 25mm buttons. Buttons shown are JHB #92847.

Required Skills:
Twisted stitches, cabling, chart reading, picking up stitches, provisional cast on (for shoulder straps; can do regular cast on instead)

Pattern Notes
The sweater body is knit from the top down, with stitches picked up from the saddle shoulder straps. Fronts and back are joined at the armholes and continued in one piece to the bottom edge.

The sleeves are worked by picking up stitches around the armhole, working short rows for the cap shaping, then continuing in the round to the wrist.

Note that the number of sts picked up along the saddles is different for the back and the fronts.
This takes into account the variance in stitch gauge between stockinette and the twisted stitch panels.
Row gauge is important. The different sizes start at different points on the main 24 row repeat to accommodate the length for that particular size. If you would like a longer sweater, it's easiest to increase or decrease the length in full 24 row increments, distributed below the armhole.

There are several ways you can distribute the additional rows. You can work any of the even sections longer (before waist decreases, after waist decreases, or after waist increases). You can also adjust the rate of the decrease or increase rows—instead of working the hip increase rows every 4th row, for example, you can work them every 5th row.

Use the knitted cast on for all cast ons unless otherwise specified.

Instructions
Saddle Straps (make 2)
Provisionally CO 18 sts. Beg on Row 1 (19, 13, 9, 19, 19, 17) of Saddle Strap chart, work until strap measures 3 (4, 4, 4½, 5, 5, 5½) in / 7.5 (10, 10, 11.5, 12.5, 12.5, 13.5)cm, ending with a WS row. Note which row you stopped on. Place sts on waste yarn; these sts will be picked up later and used for the sleeve cap.

Back
Orient straps so that the CO edges are at the neck. Pick up and knit 17 (21, 22, 22, 24, 25, 27) sts from shoulder straps with RS facing, adjusting pick-up rate as foll:
Stitches for twisted st panel, closest to neck edge (pick up at approx. 7 sts/inch): 6 (6, 5, 3, 3, 2, 0).
Stitches for St st (pick up at approx. 4¾ sts/inch): 11 (15, 17, 19, 21, 23, 27).

Work short rows and neck shaping as shown on Back Neck chart, beg with Row 2 (WS). Conceal wraps as you come to them. Use the knitted cast on for adding stitches to the back neck. Work the left shoulder first (right side of the chart) through Row 5 (RS), and place stitches on holder. Work right shoulder through Row 6, work the knitted cast-on for the back neck, then place the left stitches back onto needles with WS facing and join the two sides by continuing across the left shoulder stitches in pattern. Work through end of Back Neck chart. 80 (88, 92, 94, 100, 104, 112) sts.

When Back Neck chart is completed, continue working in pattern with Back Repeat chart. Place a marker at either side of Back Repeat panel, if desired; continue working sts outside the panel in St st. Work even in established pattern until back measures 5½ (5½, 5¾, 6, 6½, 6½, 6¾)in / 14 (14, 14.5, 15, 16.5, 16.5, 17)cm from center of shoulder strap, measured at armhole edge. End with a WS row. Note current row for reference for front armhole shaping.

Armhole shaping:
Work the following two rows 2 (3, 3, 4, 3, 4, 3) times:
(RS): K1, m1R, work in patt to 1 st before end, m1L, k1.
(WS): Work even. 84 (94, 98, 102, 106, 112, 118) sts.

Work the following two rows 1 (1, 2, 2, 2, 2, 3) times:
(RS): CO 1 st, k1, m1R, work in patt to 1 st before end, m1L, k1.
(WS): CO 1 st, work in patt to end. 88 (98, 106, 110, 114, 120,

130) sts.

Sizes XL, 2X, and 3X only, work the following two rows once:
(RS): CO 3 sts, work in patt to end.
(WS): CO 3 sts, work in patt to end. 120, 126, 136 sts.

All sizes:
Next row (RS): CO 2 (2, 3, 4, 5, 6, 6) sts, pm for side, CO 2 (2, 3, 4, 5, 6, 6) sts. Stop here; do not work remainder of row. Break yarn and set back aside on a spare needle or waste yarn. 92 (102, 112, 118, 130, 138, 148) sts. Remaining armhole shaping will be worked later, when the back and front are joined.

Right Front
With RS facing, pick up and knit 22 (25, 27, 28, 30, 32, 35) sts from edge of the right shoulder strap as foll:
Stitches for St st (pick up at 4¾ sts/inch): 3 (6, 6, 7, 8, 10, 13).
Stitches for twisted st panel (pick up at 7 sts/inch): 19 (19, 21, 21, 21, 21, 21).
Stitches for St st closest to neck (pick up at 4¾ sts/inch): 0 (0, 0, 0, 1, 1, 1).
Work as charted; see below for neckline shaping, which begins on Row 9. Note that XS & S show the initial neckline increases which are worked differently than the remainder of the neckline increases (which are worked as below). Begin working Front Panel Repeat when shoulder charts are completed; continue working sts outside the front panel in St st.

Neck shaping:
Inc 1 st at neck edge on Row 9 (RS), then every 4th row 6 (7, 8, 9, 10, 10, 10) times, then every RS row 6 (5, 5, 5, 4, 5, 6) times as foll: Unless charted differently, work in patt to 1 st before end, m1L, k1.
AT THE SAME TIME, when you reach the WS row noted for back armhole shaping, beg front armhole shaping.

Armhole shaping:
Work the following two rows 2 (3, 3, 4, 3, 4, 3) times:
(RS): K1, m1R, work in patt to end.
(WS): Work even.

Work the following two rows 1 (1, 2, 2, 2, 2, 3) times:
(RS): CO 1 st, k1, m1R, work in patt to end.
(WS): Work even.

Sizes XL, 2X, and 3X only, work the following two rows once:
(RS): CO 3 sts, work in patt to end.
(WS): Work even.

All sizes:
Next row (RS): CO 2 (2, 3, 4, 5, 6, 6) sts, pm for side, CO 2 (2, 3, 4, 5, 6, 6). 43 (47, 54, 59, 65, 71, 76) sts. Stop here; do not work remainder of row. Break yarn and set sts aside on waste yarn.

Left Front
With RS facing, pick up and knit 22 (25, 27, 28, 30, 32, 35) sts from edge of the left shoulder strap, distributing sts as for right shoulder. Work as charted, beginning neck shaping on Row 9. Begin working Front Panel repeats when shoulder charts are completed; continue working sts outside panel in St st.

Neck shaping:
Note: As before, the initial increases for sizes XS and S are charted. Once those are completed, worked the remainder as below.

Inc 1 st at neck edge on Row 9 (RS), then every 4th row 6 (7, 8, 9, 10, 10, 10) times, then every RS row 6 (5, 5, 5, 4, 5, 6) times as foll: K1, m1R, work in patt to end.
AT THE SAME TIME, when you reach the WS row noted for back armhole shaping, beg front armhole shaping.

Armhole shaping:
Work the following two rows 2 (3, 3, 4, 3, 4, 3) times:
(RS): Work in patt to 1 st before end, m1L, k1.
(WS): Work even.

Work the following two rows 1 (1, 2, 2, 2, 2, 3) times:
(RS): Work in patt to 1 st before end, m1L, k1.
(WS): CO 1 st, work in patt to end.

Sizes XL, 2X, and 3X only, work the following two rows once:
(RS): Work even.
(WS): CO 3 sts, work in patt to end.

All sizes:
After all shaping is complete, there are 39 (43, 48, 51, 55, 59, 64) sts.

Main Body
With RS of Left Front facing you, work in pattern to end, join to back, work across back in pattern, join to Right Front, work in pattern to end. 174 (192, 214, 228, 250, 268, 288) sts.

Work even for 2½ (2½, 2¼, 2, 2½, 2¾, 3)in / 6.5 (6.5, 5.5, 5, 6.5, 7, 7.5)cm, ending with a WS row.

Waist shaping, decreases:
Row 1 (RS): Knit to first front panel, work panel, k2tog, knit to 2 sts before back panel, ssk, work panel, k2tog, work to 2 sts before second front panel, ssk, work panel, knit to end. 4 sts dec'd.
Rows 2-3: Work even.
Row 4 (WS): Purl to first front panel, work panel, p2tog, purl to 2 sts before back panel, p2tog tbl, work panel, p2tog, work to 2 sts before second front panel, p2tog tbl, work panel, purl to end. 4 sts dec'd.
Rows 5-6: Work even.
Rep Rows 1-6 once more, then Row 1 only once. 154 (172, 194, 108, 230, 248, 268) sts.
Work even for 2½ (2½, 2¼, 2, 2½, 2¾, 3)in / 6.5 (6.5, 5.5, 5, 6.5, 7, 7.5)cm, ending with a WS row.

Waist shaping, increases:
Read ahead: Border charts are worked simultaneously with waist increases.
Row 1 (RS): Knit to first front panel, work panel, k1, m1L, work to 1 st before back panel, m1R, k1, work panel, k1, m1L, work to 1 st before second front panel, m1R, k1, work panel, knit to end. 4 sts inc'd.
Rows 2-4: Work even.
Rep Rows 1-4 5 times more. 178 (196, 218, 232, 254, 272, 292) sts.

AT THE SAME TIME, when body measures approx. 8¼ (8, 7¾, 7,

8, 8½, 9½)in / 20.5 (20, 19.5, 18, 20, 21.5, 23.5)cm from underarm ending on Row 24 of Panel Repeat charts, begin working Front and Back Border charts.

When Border charts are complete, work 3 rows in St st, 2 rows in reverse St st, then 3 rows in St st. BO knitwise. Fold hem under and sew.

Sleeves

Note for Saddle Strap Chart: Simply knit the first and last sts rather than slipping them. These stitches are not shown on the sleeve border charts.

Starting from the underarm center and going in a clockwise direction, pick up (do not knit, just pick up) 21 (23, 25, 30, 32, 35, 37) stitches, place 18 stitches from the shoulder straps on needle, pick up 21 (23, 25, 30, 32, 35, 37) stitches. Pm for beginning of round at underarm center. 60 (64, 68, 78, 82, 88, 92) sts.

Work short rows to shape sleeve cap as described below, but do NOT conceal wraps.

Short Row 1 (RS): Join yarn beginning at stitch 20 (21, 23, 26, 27, 29, 31); work in St st to shoulder strap, work shoulder strap in pattern, work in St st to stitch 41 (44, 46, 53, 56, 60, 62), wrap next st, turn.

Short Row 2 (WS): Work in pattern back to and including first stitch worked, wrap next st, turn.

Short Rows 3 & 4: Work in pattern to wrapped st, work wrapped st, wrap next st, turn.

Repeat Short Rows 3 & 4 until 5 (6, 8, 10, 11, 13, 13) sts remain unworked between last wrapped st and the marker, ending with a WS row.

Turn and begin working in the round.

Work in the round in pattern until sleeve measures 5 (5½, 6, 6¾, 7¼, 7¾, 8¾)in / 12.5 (14, 15, 17, 18.5, 20, 22.5)cm from shoulder. Dec 1 st at each end of next rnd, then every foll 12th (12th, 11th, 7th, 7th, 6th, 5th) rnd 8 (8, 9, 13, 14, 16, 16) more times as foll: K1, k2tog, work to 3 sts before end, ssk, k1. 42 (46, 48, 50, 52, 54, 58) sts.

Work even until sleeve measures approx. 18 (18¾, 19¾, 19¾, 21¼, 21¼, 21¼)in / 45 (47, 49.5, 49.5, 53, 53, 53)cm from shoulder, ending with Rnd 24 of Saddle Strap chart.

Work Sleeve Border chart. When Sleeve Border chart is complete, knit 3 rnds, purl 2 rnds, knit 3 rnds. BO.

Collar and Button Band

Beginning at bottom right front edge, RS facing, pick up and knit 91 (91, 91, 88, 91, 94, 97) sts to neck shaping, PM, pick up and knit 34 (37, 40, 43, 46, 48, 51) sts to saddle strap, remove waste yarn from provisional CO, place 18 saddle strap sts onto needles and knit them, pick up and knit 51 (51, 54, 52, 57, 59, 59) sts to saddle strap, work second saddle strap same as first, pick up and knit 34 (37, 40, 43, 46, 48, 51) sts to end of neck shaping, PM, up and knit 91 (91, 88, 88, 91, 94, 97) sts to end.

Rib set-up row (WS): (P1 tbl, k2) to 1 st before marker, p1tbl, sm, (p2, k1 tbl) to 2 sts before marker, p2, sm, (p1 tbl, k2) to 1 st before end, p1tbl.

Begin collar shaping:
Short Row 1 (RS): Sl1, work in pattern to 1 st before second marker, wrap next st, turn.

Short Row 2 (WS): Work in pattern to 1 st before first marker, wrap next st, turn.

Short Rows 3 & 4: Work in patt to 6 sts before last wrapped st, wrap next st, turn.

Rep Short Rows 3 & 4 another 4 (7, 0, 3, 1, 3, 6) times.

Short Rows 5 & 6: Work in patt to 5 sts before last wrapped st, wrap next st, turn.

Rep Short Rows 5 & 6 another 3 (0, 9, 6, 9, 7, 4) times.

After completing short rows, work in pattern to end, concealing wraps as you come to them.

Work even until button band measures ½ (½, ¾, ¾, ¾, ¾, ¾)in / 2 (2, 2.5, 2.5, 2.5, 2.5, 2.5)cm, ending with a WS row.

Work buttonholes along right front as follows:

Next row (RS): [K1 tbl, p2] 7 (7, 7, 6, 7, 7, 8) times, *ssk, yo twice, k2tog, p2, [k1 tbl, p2] 4 times; rep from * twice more, ssk, yo twice, k2tog, continue in patt to end.

Next row (WS): Work in patt, working (k1 tbl, p1 tbl) into each double yo from previous row.

Next row: Work in established ribbing.

Continue in patt until button band measures 1½ (1½, 2, 2, 2, 2, 2)in / 4 (4, 5, 5, 5, 5, 5)cm. BO in pattern.

Finishing

Weave in all ends. Block. Sew on buttons. Whipstitch around buttonholes if desired.

Saddle Strap chart

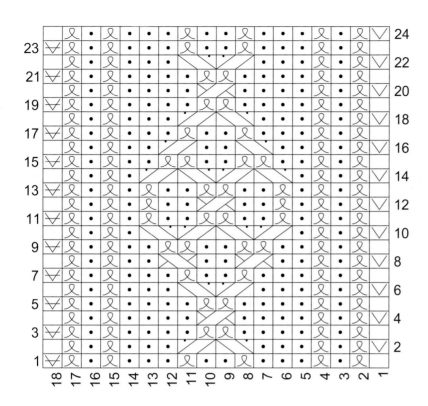

Sleeve Border

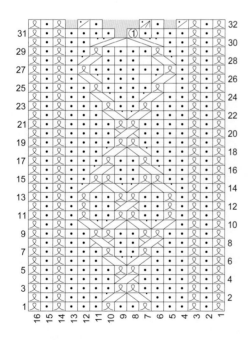

	1/1 RC
	1/1 LC
	RS & WS: 1/1 RPC
	RS & WS: 1/1 LPC
	1/2 LPC
	1/2 RPC
	s1
	WS: s1
	RS: p2tog; WS: k2tog
	RS: p3tog; WS: k3tog
W	w&t

		RS: k; WS: p
•		RS: p; WS: k
Ꝺ		RS: k-tbl; WS: p-tbl
KCO		RS & WS: Knitted cast on.
PUK		Pick up and knit.
①		RS: Cable Decr; WS: Cable Decr: Slip the next 2 sts to the RH needle. Pass the first stitch over the second stitch. Move stitch back to LH needle. Purl that stitch.

XS Left Front Shoulder

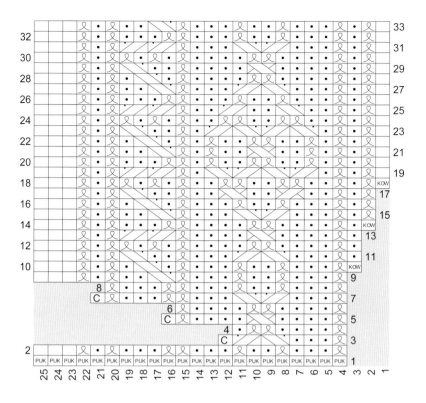

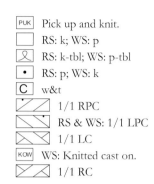

PUK		Pick up and knit.
		RS: k; WS: p
ℓ		RS: k-tbl; WS: p-tbl
•		RS: p; WS: k
C		w&t
		1/1 RPC
		RS & WS: 1/1 LPC
		1/1 LC
KOW		WS: Knitted cast on.
		1/1 RC

XS Right Front Shoulder

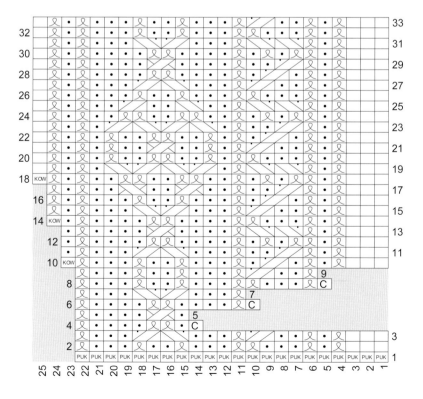

S BACK NECK

S LEFT FRONT SHOULDER

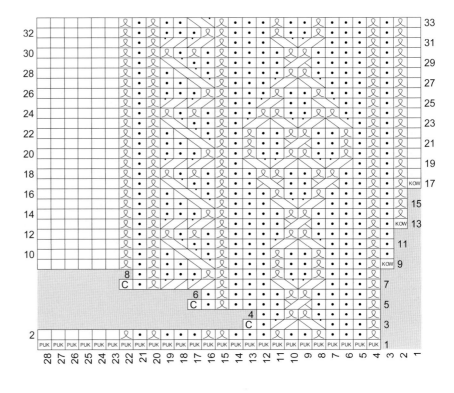

S RIGHT FRONT SHOULDER

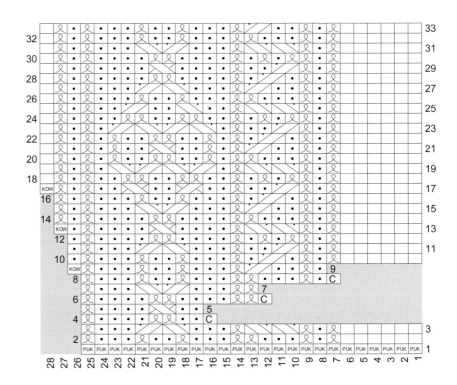

PUK	Pick up and knit.
ᛘ	RS: k;tWbl S: p;tW
•	RS: pbl S: k
☐	RS: kbl S: p
⟋	RS w 1 S: &&RP/
⟍	&&CP/
C	1 S: Lwt
⟋	&&C/
KOW	Knitted cast on.
⟍	&&R/

M Back Neck

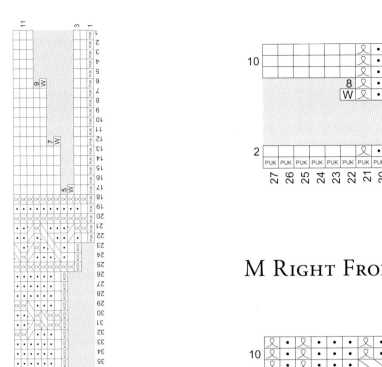

M Left Front Shoulder

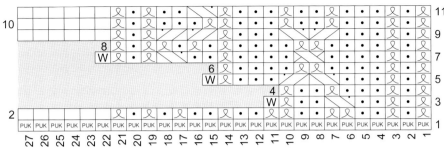

M Right Front Shoulder

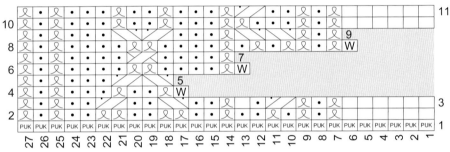

PUK	Pick up and knit.	
	RS: k-tbl; WS: p-tbl	
•	RS: p; WS: k	
	RS: k; WS: p	
	1/1 RPC	
	1/1 LPC	
W	WS: w&t	
	1/1 RC	

L Back Neck

L Left Front Shoulder

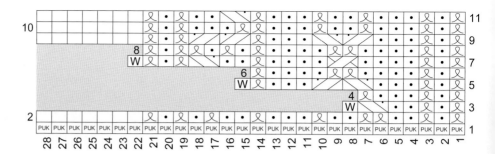

L Right Front Shoulder

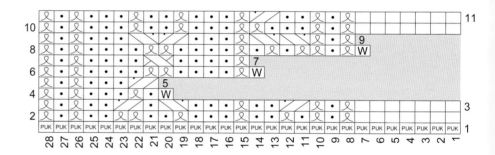

PUK	Pick up and knit.
	RS: k-tbl; WS: p-tbl
•	RS: p; WS: k
	RS: k; WS: p
	1/1 RPC
	1/1 LPC
W	WS: w&t
	1/1 LC

XL Back Neck

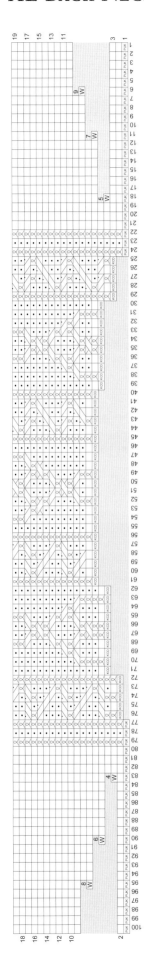

XL Left Front Shoulder

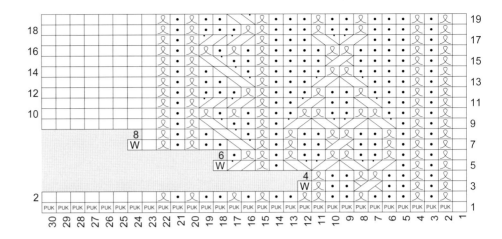

XL Right Front Shoulder

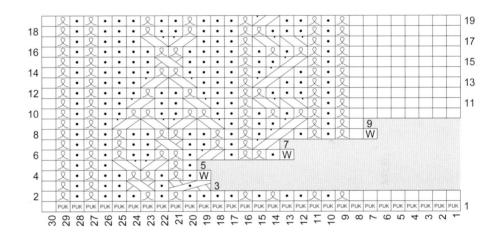

	Pick up ida
PUK	nd k alRS: k Sdb
⅄	Pick l-; Wp idal-; W
•	Pidaup ick
⤫	1/1kCL
⤢	1/1/1kPLat
W	p idav&-
⟋	1/1kCnL
⟋	Pik&dp ickl/1kPnL

2X BACK NECK

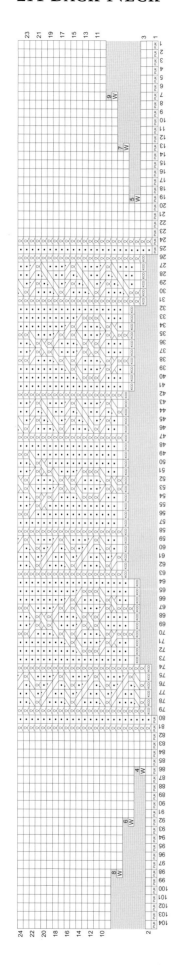

2X LEFT FRONT SHOULDER

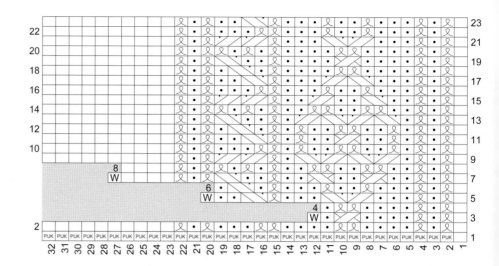

2X RIGHT FRONT SHOULDER

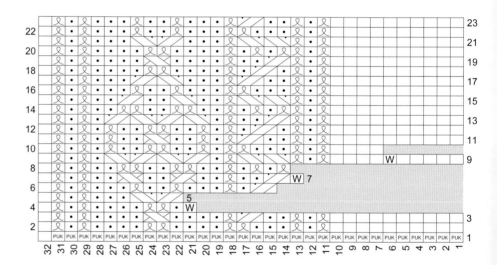

☐	Pick up i da
PUK	nd k al RS: k S db
⚇	Pick 1-; Wp i da l-; W
•	Pi da u kp i dk
⤬	1/1kCL
⤬	Pi kw kp i dd /1kPnL
W	Pi kw kp i de&w-
⤬	1/1kCnL
⤬	1/1kPL

3x BACK NECK

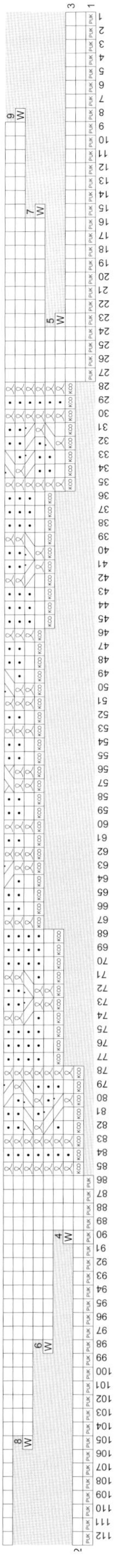

3x LEFT FRONT SHOULDER

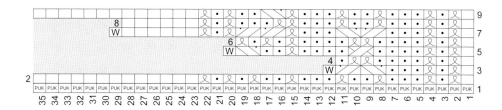

3x RIGHT FRONT SHOULDER

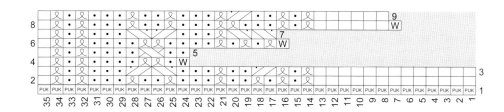

| PUK | Pick up and knit. |
| RS: k- b S: p |
| RS: klt; Wb S: plt; W |
| • | RS: p- b S: k |
| 1/1 RPC |
| 1/1 LPC |
| W | b S: w&t |
| 1/1 LC |

SCHEMATIC FOR ALL SIZES

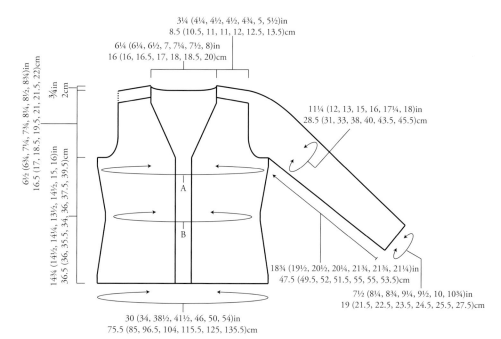

3¼ (4¼, 4½, 4½, 4¾, 5, 5½)in
8.5 (10.5, 11, 11, 12, 12.5, 13.5)cm

6¼ (6¼, 6½, 7, 7¼, 7½, 8)in
16 (16, 16.5, 17, 18, 18.5, 20)cm

¾in
2cm

6½ (6¾, 7¼, 7¾, 8¼, 8½, 8¾)in
16.5 (17, 18.5, 19.5, 21, 21.5, 22)cm

14¾ (14½, 14¼, 13½, 14½, 15, 16)in
36.5 (36, 35.5, 34, 36, 37.5, 39.5)cm

11¼ (12, 13, 15, 16, 17¼, 18)in
28.5 (31, 33, 38, 40, 43.5, 45.5)cm

A

B

18¾ (19½, 20½, 20¼, 21¾, 21¾, 21¼)in
47.5 (49.5, 52, 51.5, 55, 55, 53.5)cm

7½ (8¼, 8¾, 9¼, 9½, 10, 10¾)in
19 (21.5, 22.5, 23.5, 24.5, 25.5, 27.5)cm

30 (34, 38½, 41½, 46, 50, 54)in
75.5 (85, 96.5, 104, 115.5, 125, 135.5)cm

A:
29¼ (33¼, 37¾, 40¾, 45¼, 49¼, 53¼)in
73.5 (83, 94.5, 102, 113.5, 123, 133.5)cm

B:
25 (29, 33½, 36½, 41, 45, 49)in
63 (72.5, 84, 91.5, 103, 112.5, 123)cm

73

BACK REPEAT CHART

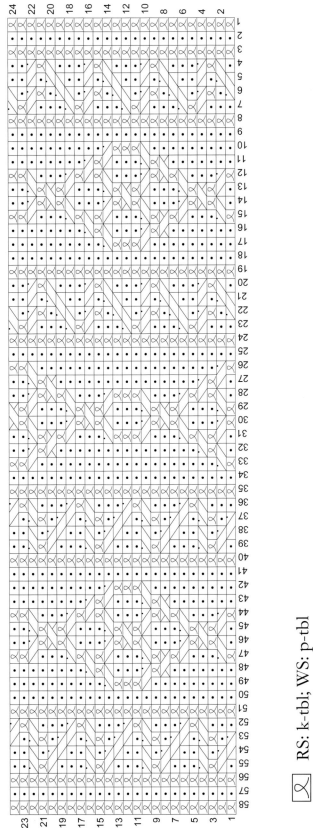

⌀ RS: k-tbl; WS: p-tbl

• RS: p; WS: k

⟋ RS & WS: 1/1 LPC

⟍ RS & WS: 1/1 RPC

⟋ 1/1 RC

⟍ 1/1 LC

Side repeat charts

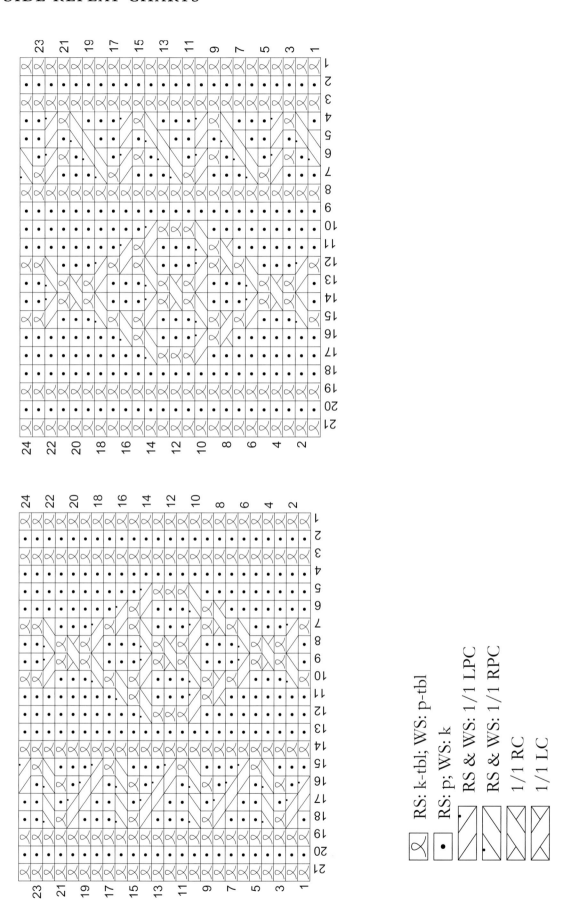

RS: k-tbl; WS: p-tbl

RS: p; WS: k

RS & WS: 1/1 LPC

RS & WS: 1/1 RPC

1/1 RC

1/1 LC

RIGHT SIDE REPEAT CHART

LEFT SIDE REPEAT CHART

Back border chart

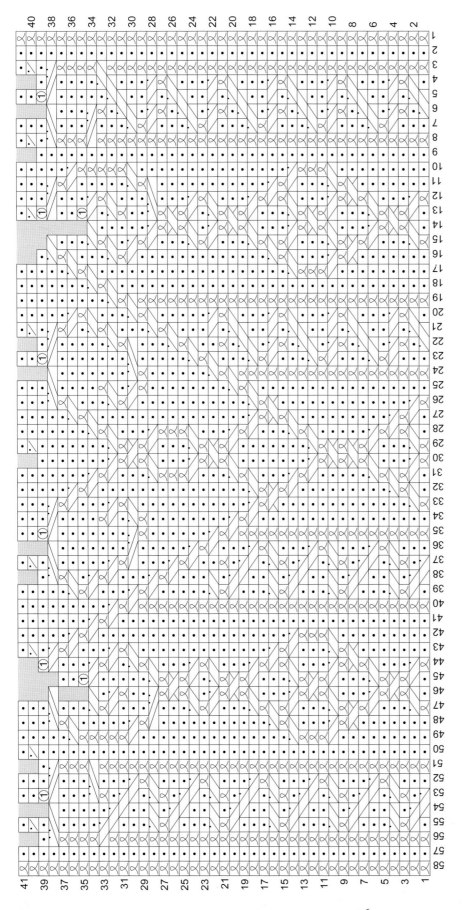

RS: k-tbl; WS: p-tbl

RS: p; WS: k

RS & WS: 1/1 LPC

RS & WS: 1/1 RPC

1/1 LC

1/1 RC

1/2 LPC

1/2 RPC

① WS: Cable Decr: Slip the next 2 sts to the RH needle. Pass the first stitch over the second stitch. Move stitch back to LH needle. Purl that stitch.

① p2tog

Side border chart

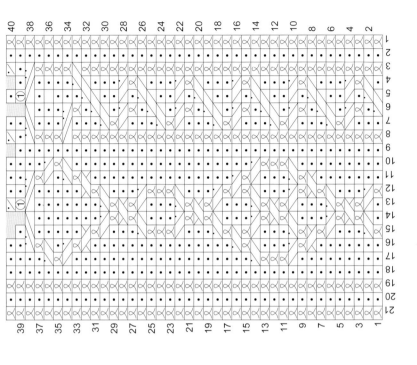

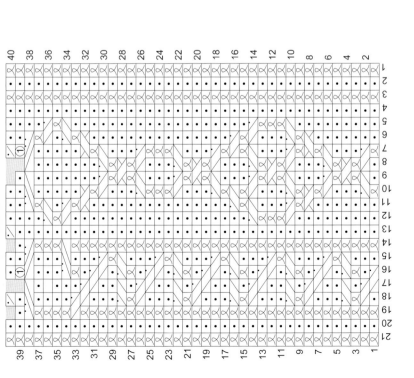

⊠	RS: k-tbl; WS: p-tbl
•	RS: p; WS: k
	RS & WS: 1/1 LPC
	1/1 RPC
	1/1 LC
	1/1 RC
	1/2 RPC
k	
	1/2 LPC
①	WS: Cable Decr: Slip the next 2 sts to the RH needle. Pass the first stitch over the second stitch. Move stitch back to LH needle. Purl that stitch.
	p2tog

Left Side Border Chart

Right Side Border Chart

77

Wrought Mitts

These mitts were the first of the Wrought patterns, and their motif the guideline for all the others. I love the curls and curves you can obtain with the traveling stitches.

Size
One, to fit up to 8in / 20.5cm hand circumference

Finished Measurements
6½"/ 16.5cm palm circumference, unstretched. Easily stretches to fit 8" circumference.

Yarn
Stricken Smitten BFL & Silk Fingering, 45% silk/55% Bluefaced Leicester wool, 430 yds / 100g, 1 skein in Braeburn

Needles
US 1 (2.25mm) circular(s) or double pointed as preferred, or size to obtain gauge.

Gauge
36 sts and 52 rnds = 4in / 10cm in stockinette stitch

Notions & Other Supplies
Yarn needle, waste yarn, 3 stitch markers, cable needle if you use one.

Required Skills
Chart reading, twisted stitches, cabling, knitting in the round.

Instructions
CO 55 sts. Join in the round, being careful not to twist. PM for beginning of round.
Purl 5 rnds.
Knit 3 rnds.
Begin chart. Work as charted until Rnd 40. At this point, the k tbl with the yellow background are worked only for the left mitt, and the k tbl with the magenta background are worked only for the right mitt. Simply knit these stitches for the opposite mitt.
On Rnd 40 of chart, set up for thumb gusset:
Right Mitt: Work through stitch column 43 of chart, pm, m1, pm, work to end.
Left Mitt: Work through stitch column 68 of chart, pm, m1, pm, work to end.
Note the gusset sts are worked between the columns of k tbl sts.

Thumb Gusset
Rnd 1: Work as charted to marker, sm, m1r, k to marker, m1l, sm, work to end.
Rnds 2 &3: Work as charted to first gusset marker, sm, k to second gusset marker, sm, work to end.
Repeat above 3 rounds until you have 25 sts between markers, ending on Rnd 3 (chart Rnd 76).
Next rnd: Work as charted to first gusset marker, remove marker,

place the 25 gusset sts on waste yarn, use the backward loop method to CO 4 sts, remove second gusset marker, work to end.

Remainder of Mitt
Complete chart. Note the 5 with the magenta background applies only to the right mitt and the 5 with the yellow background to the left mitt. These symbols take into account the sts cast on after separation for the thumb gusset.
Purl 2 rnds. Knit 3 rnds. Purl 5 rnds. BO purlwise.

Thumb
Place 25 gusset sts back onto needles. Pick up and knit 4 sts from edge of opening, pm for beginning of rnd, pick up and knit 4 sts, then knit gusset stitches. 33 sts.
Rnds 1 & 2: K1, k2tog, k to 3 sts before end, ssk, k1. 29 sts.
Rnd 3: P1, p2tog, p to 3 sts before end, p2tog, p1. 27 sts.
Rnds 4-7: Purl.
BO purlwise.

Finishing
Weave in ends. Block.

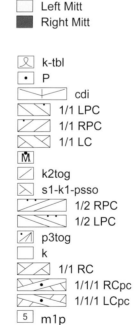

☐	Left Mitt
■	Right Mitt

	k-tbl
•	P
	cdi
	1/1 LPC
	1/1 RPC
	1/1 LC
M	
	k2tog
	s1-k1-psso
	1/2 RPC
	1/2 LPC
	p3tog
	k
	1/1 RC
	1/1/1 RCpc
	1/1/1 LCpc
5	m1p

WROUGHT BERET

This cozy beret can also be worn as a beanie—just block it flat rather than over a plate.

Size
One size, average woman's, to fit head circumference 21-23"/ 53.5-58.5cm

Finished measurements
Brim circumference 18"/ 45.5cm

Yarn
Shibui Merino Alpaca, 50% alpaca/50% merino, heavy worsted, 132 yds / 100 gms, 2 skeins, Burgundy

Needles
US 6 (4.00mm), or size to obtain gauge. Your choice of Magic Loop, 2 circulars or DPNs.
US 5 (3.75mm) for ribbing, or one size smaller than for body of beret.

Gauge
20 sts and 28 rounds = 4" in stockinette stitch

Notions
Yarn needle, 5 stitch markers (one unique for beginning of round), cable needle if you use one

Skills needed
Knitting in the round, chart reading, twisted stitches, cabling

Ribbing
CO 90 sts. Join in the round, being careful not to twist. PM for beginning of round. Work in [k tbl twice, p1] ribbing for 15 rounds.

Body of Beret
Next round: [M1p, p3] to end of round. (120 sts)
Begin working chart, working 5 repeats of chart around, placing markers at the end of each repeat if desired. Complete chart.

Finishing
Cut yarn, leaving a tail & thread through remaining stitches. Pull tightly to close top of hat. Weave in loose ends. Block.

WROUGHT BERET CHART

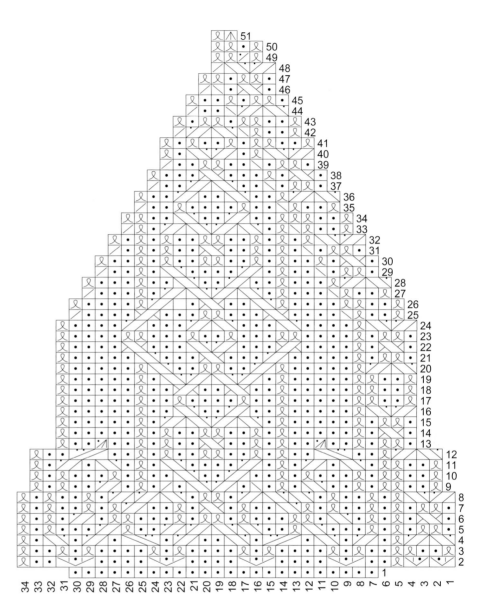

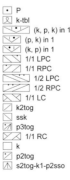

•	P
ደ	k-tbl
	(k, p, k) in 1
	(p, k) in 1
	(k, p) in 1
	1/1 LPC
	1/1 RPC
	1/2 LPC
	1/2 RPC
	1/1 LC
	k2tog
	ssk
	p3tog
	1/1 RC
	k
	p2tog
	s2tog-k1-p2sso

Wrought Socks

Worked cuff down, these socks carry through with the ironwork motifs, even along the heel flap.

Size

S (M, L)

Finished Measurements

7½ (8, 8½)in / 19 (20.5, 21.5)cm foot circumference. These are stretchy because of the ribbing and twisted stitch pattern.

Yarn

The Sanguine Gryphon Bugga!, 70% superwash merino/20% cashmere/10% nylon, 412 yd /113g, 1 skein in Adonis Butterfly

Needles

US 1 (2.25mm) circular(s) or double pointed as preferred, or size to obtain gauge.

Gauge

32 sts and 40 rnds = 4in / 10cm in stockinette stitch

Notions & Other Supplies

Yarn needle, minimum 3 stitch markers (one unique for beginning of round), cable needle if you use one.

Skills Required

Twisted stitches, working in the round, picking up stitches, Kitchener stitch, cables.

Instructions

Cuff and Leg

Cast on 60 (64, 68) sts. Join for working in the round, being careful not to twist. PM for beginning of round. Work front then back chart in your size. Complete Rnds 1-41.

Heel Flap

Row 42: Work front chart sts then reserve these stitches for the instep. Work Rnd 42 of Back chart. Turn.

Work Heel Flap chart Rows 1-10, then repeat Rows 9 and 10 until you have 15 (16, 17) selvedge stitches on each side of flap.

Turn Heel

Row 1 (WS): Sl1, p16 (18, 20), p2tog, p1, turn.
Row 2: Sl1, k5 (7, 9), ssk, k1, turn.
Row 3: Sl1, purl until 1 st before the gap, p2tog, p1, turn.
Row 4: Sl1, knit until 1 st before the gap, ssk, k1, turn.
Rep Rows 3 and 4 until all sts at either end are used up. Do not turn on the last row. 18 (20, 22) sts remain.

Gusset

Pick up and knit 15 (16, 17) sts along side of heel flap, pm for instep, work Rnd 43 of Front chart, pm for instep, pick up and knit 15 (16,

17) sts along side of heel flap. K9 (10, 11) sts, pm to mark new beg of rnd. 78 (84, 90) sts.

Next rnd: Knit to marker, sm, work next rnd of Front chart, sm, knit to end.

Dec rnd: Knit to 2 sts before instep marker, k2tog, sm, work chart, sm, ssk, knit to end.

Rep these two rnds until 60 (64, 68) sts rem.

Foot

Continue working the instep in pattern and sole in St st through end of chart, then work St st over all sts until foot measures 2in / 5cm less than desired finished length.

Toe

Rnd 1: Knit.
Rnd 2: Knit to last 2 sole sts, k2tog, ssk, knit to last 2 instep sts, k2tog, ssk, knit to end.
Rep these two rnds until 20 (24, 28) sts rem. Knit to end of sole sts. Use Kitchener stitch to graft the toe sts together.

Finishing

Weave in any loose ends. Block.

SMALL HEEL FLAP

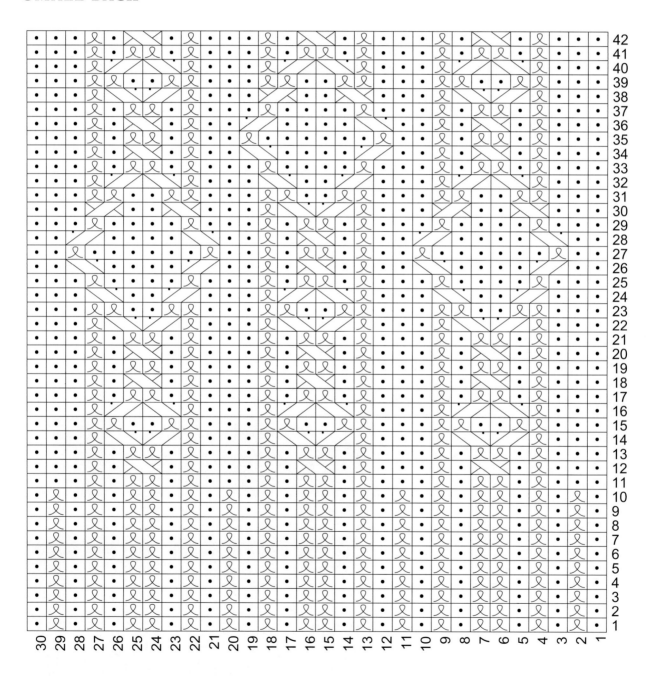

SMALL BACK

SMALL FRONT

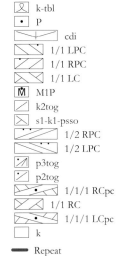

	k-tbl
•	P
	cdi
	1/1 LPC
	1/1 RPC
	1/1 LC
M	M1P
	k2tog
	s1-k1-psso
	1/2 RPC
	1/2 LPC
	p3tog
	p2tog
	1/1/1 RCpc
	1/1 RC
	1/1/1 LCpc
	k
▬	Repeat

Medium heel flap

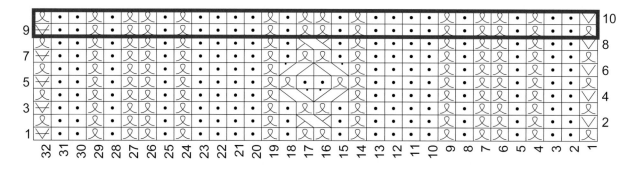

Medium back

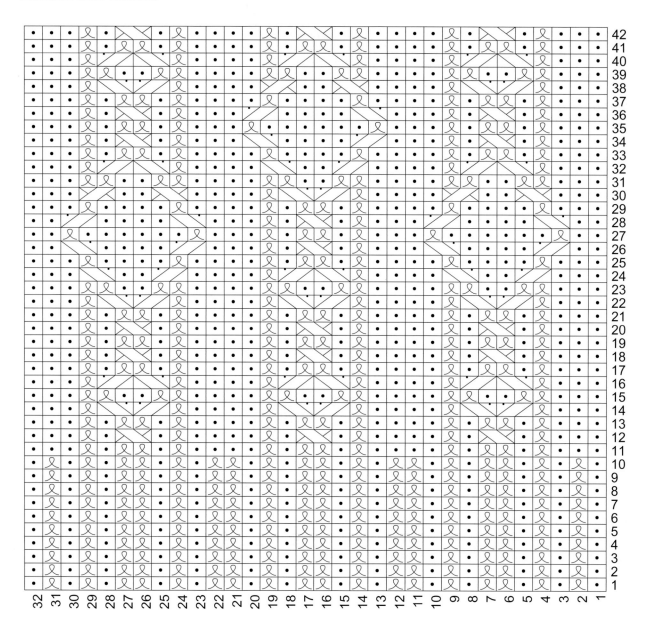

Medium front

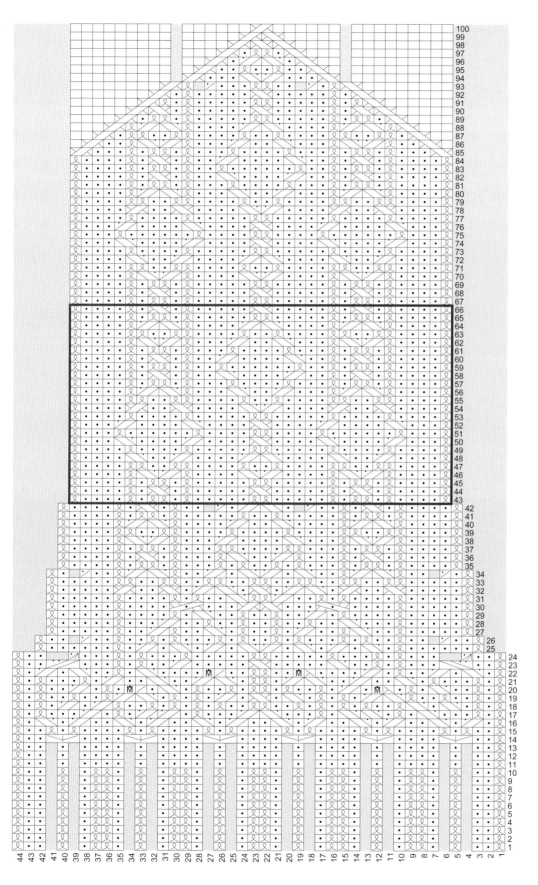

	k-tbl
•	P
	cdi
	1/1 LPC
	1/1 RPC
	1/1 LC
M̄	M1P
	k2tog
	s1-k1-psso
	1/2 RPC
	1/2 LPC
	p3tog
	p2tog
	1/1/1 RCpc
	1/1 RC
	1/1/1 LCpc
	k
▬	Repeat

LARGE HEEL FLAP

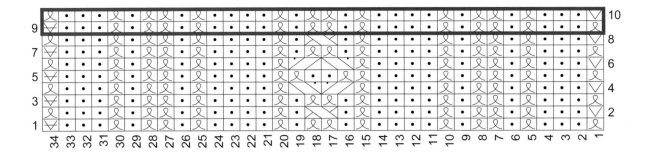

LARGE BACK

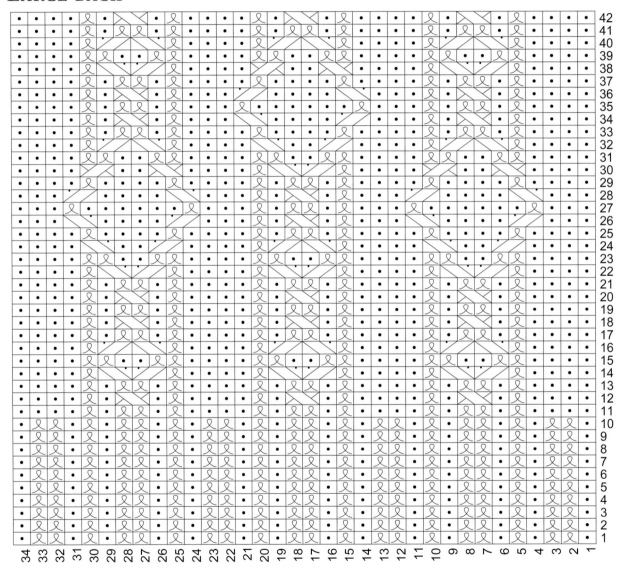

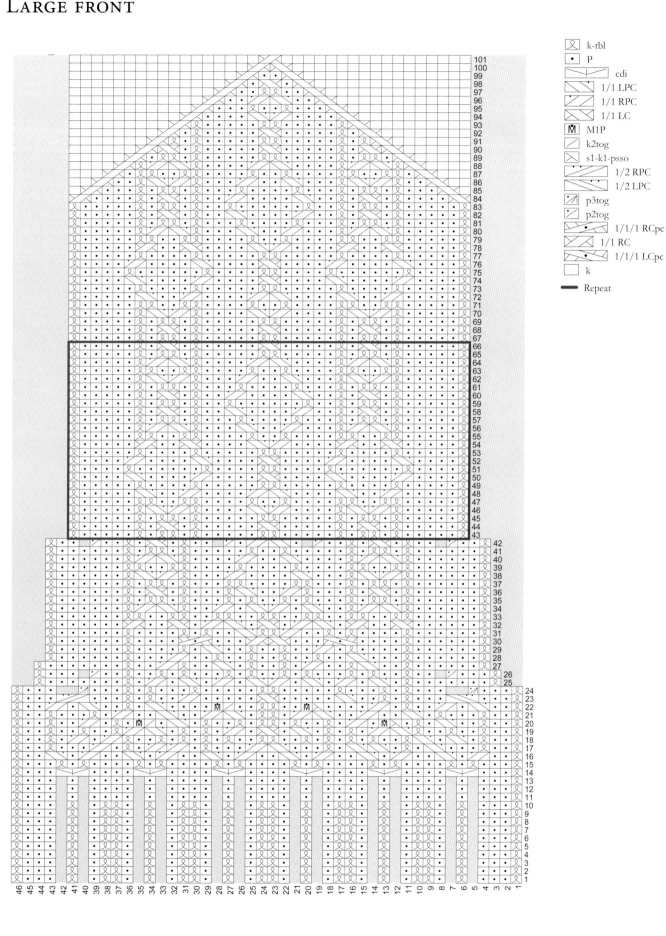

QUATREFOIL FINGERLESS MITTS

> *Quatrefoil motifs are common in decorative iron and metal pieces. Here I've created a quatrefoil motif perfect for beginners to stranded knitting; in only one instance (working across the thumb gusset) do you ever carry a strand more than 1". You can work the mitts in bold contrasting colors, such as the full mittens, or in a more subtle colorway. Fingerless mitt instructions are given here; for full mitten pattern, see page 104.*

Size
S/M (M/L), to fit hand circumference 7½ (8½)in / 19 (21.5)cm

Finished Measurements
Hand circumference 8 (9)in / 20.5 (23)cm

Yarn
MacKintosh Yarns Skye Sock Yarn, 100% superwash merino, 368 yds / 115g, 1 skein each Skyshatter (MC) and Twilight (CC).

Needles
US 1½ (2.5mm) circular(s) or double pointed, as preferred, or size to obtain gauge.

Gauge
32 sts and 44 rnds = 4in /10cm in stranded stockinette stitch

Notions & Other Supplies
Yarn needle, 3 stitch markers (one unique for beg of rnd), waste yarn, spare circular for provisional CO (optional).

Required Skills
Knitting in the round, stranded knitting, provisional cast on, sewn hem, chart reading.

Pattern Notes
You can work a plain hem by purling the entire turning round rather than [yo, k2tog].

Picot Hem
Provisionally CO 64 (72) sts in MC. Join in the round, being careful not to twist. PM for beginning of round.
Knit 7 rnds.
Picot rnd: *Yo, k2tog; rep from * to end.
Knit 7 rnds.
Fold cuff with wrong sides facing. If you used waste yarn rather than an extra circular needle for your provisional cast on, place those stitches on a needle now and hold behind the working needle.
Next rnd: *Knit 1 from front needle tog with 1 from back needle; rep from * to end.
Knit 4 rounds in MC.

Remainder of Cuff & Hand
Work Rnds 1-11 of Right or Left Mitten Chart.

Rnd 12:
Right Mitten: Work through stitch 33 (37) as charted, pm for thumb gusset, work 1 as charted, pm for thumb gusset, work to end of round.
Left Mitten: Work through stitch 30 (34) as charted, pm for thumb gusset, work 1 as charted, pm for thumb gusset, work to end of round.
Continue working in pattern, slipping markers as you reach them. When you have completed the thumb gusset portion of the chart, on the next rnd (chart Rnd 43) place the 27 thumb stitches on waste yarn as indicated, CO 1 st using the backward loop cast on method, and continue working the rest of the mitten chart. 64 (72) sts.

Upper Hem
After completing the chart, knit 5 rounds in MC.
Picot rnd: *Yo, k2tog; rep from * to end.
Knit 5 rnds.
Cut yarn, leaving a yarn tail with a length of 3x the diameter of the mitten.
Fold the top edge of the mitten, wrong sides facing, and sew/weave through each live stitch and its corresponding purl bump such that the picot edge remains even. Do not pull too tightly.

Thumb
Replace 27 thumb sts onto your needles. Pick up and knit 4 sts from edge of opening then work to end of rnd. PM for beg of rnd. 31 sts.
Complete chart.
Switch to MC.
Knit 5 rnds.
Picot rnd: *Yo, k2tog; rep from * to end.
Knit 5 rnds.
Fold with wrong sides facing and sew (see the mitten hem directions above) the live sts to the inside of the thumb.

Finishing
Weave in loose ends. Block.

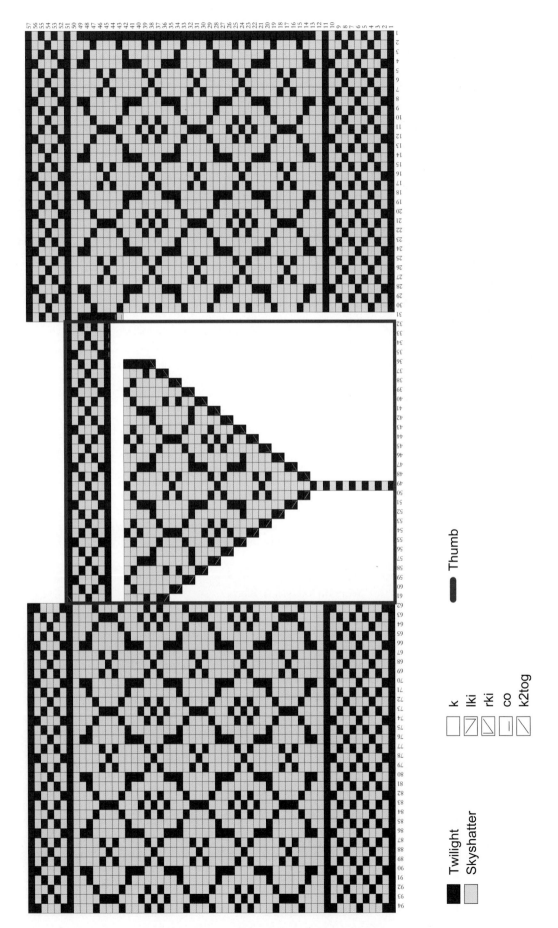

Thumb

k
lki
rki
co
k2tog

Twilight
Skyshatter

S/M Fingerless Mitt Right

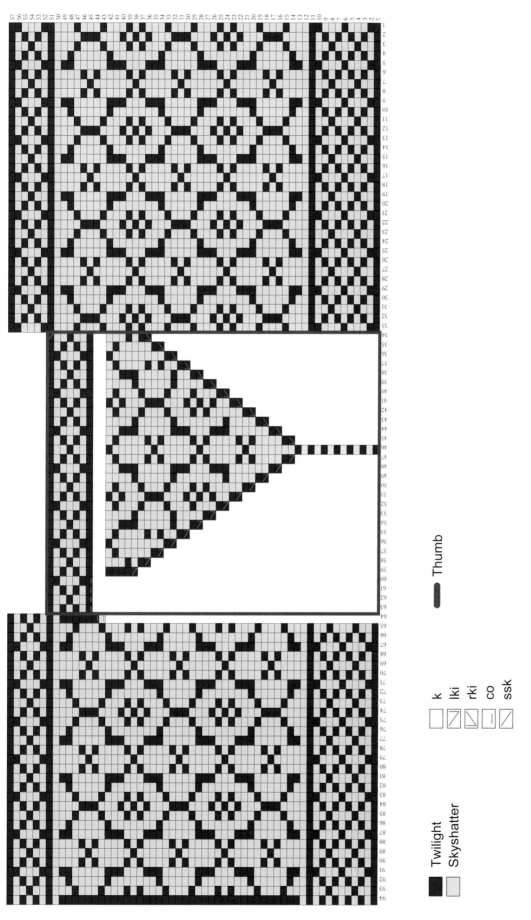

● Thumb

k — ⬜
lki — ◪
rki — ◩
co — ⬓
ssk — ◪

■ Twilight
⬜ Skyshatter

M/L Fingerless Mitt Left

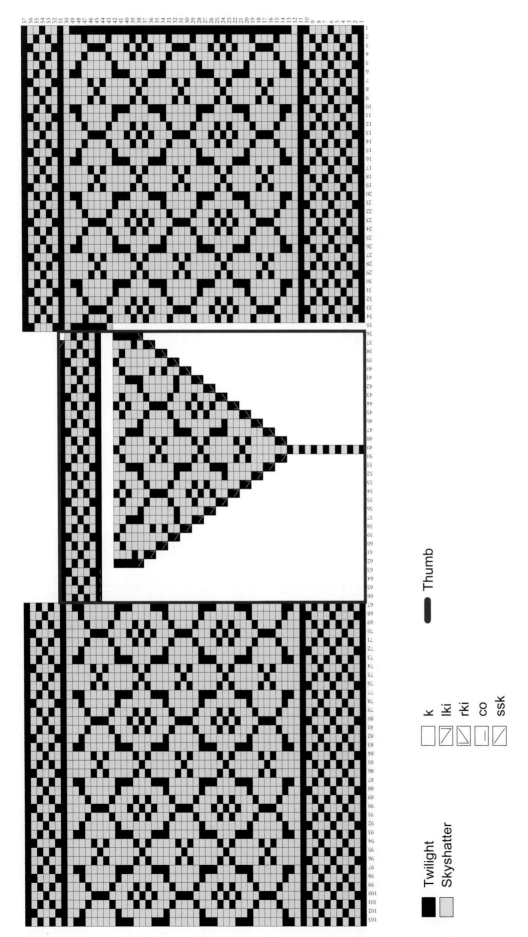

Thumb

k

lki

rki

co

ssk

Twilight

Skyshatter

M/L Fingerless Mitt Right

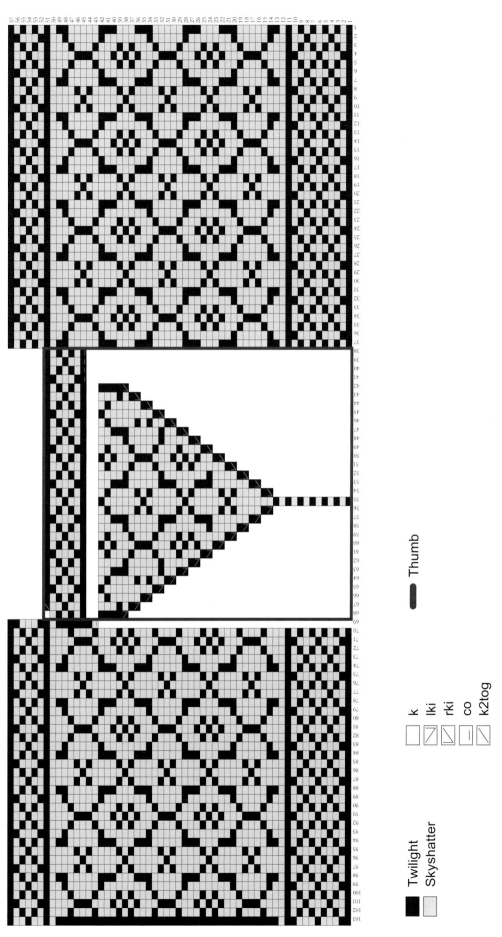

Thumb

k lki rki co k2tog

Twilight
Skyshatter

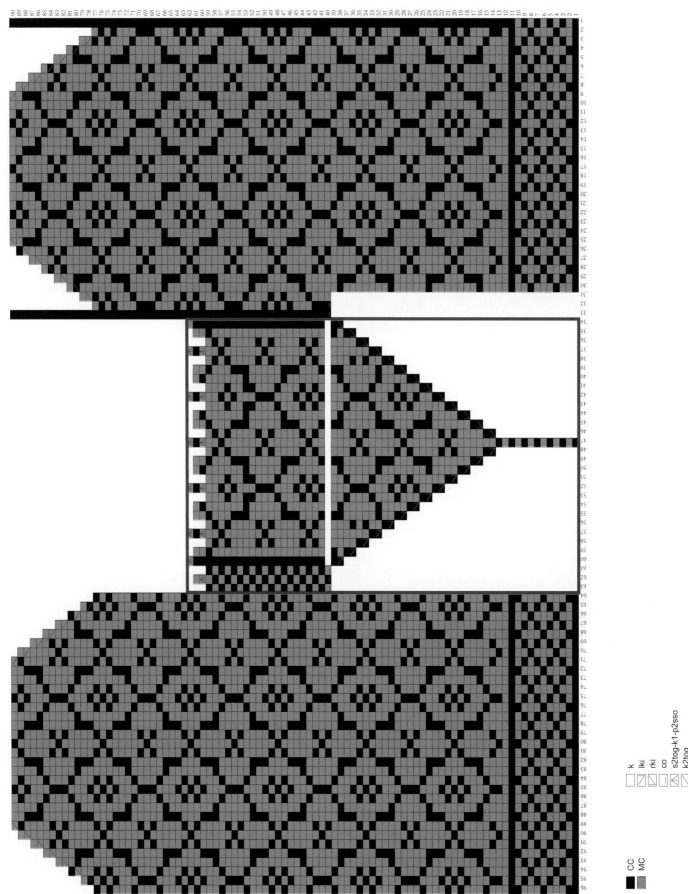

S/M Mitt Right

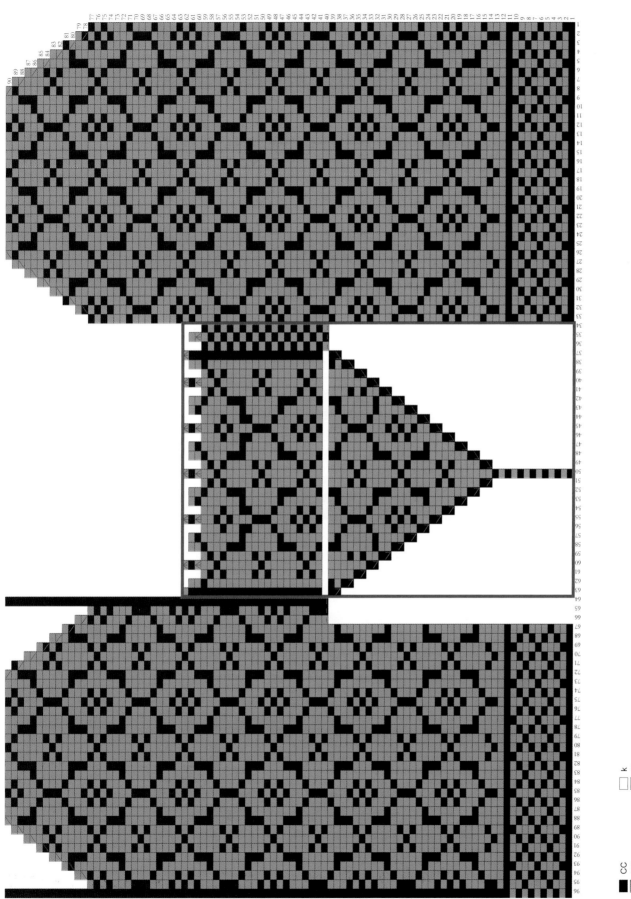

k
lki
rki
co
s2tog-k1-p2sso
k2tog
ssk

CC
MC

M/L Mitt Left

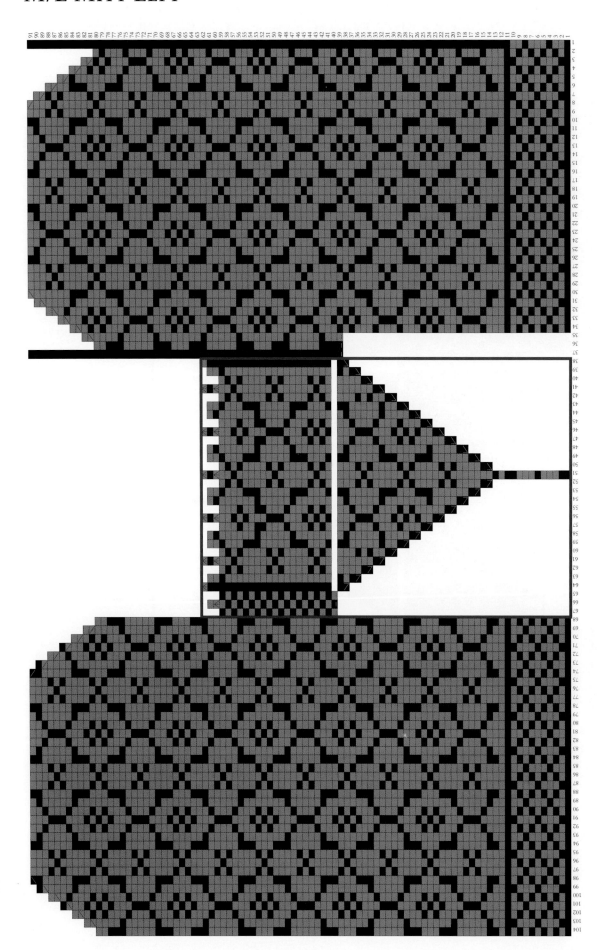

k
lki
rki
co
s2tog-k1-p2sso
k2tog
ssk

CC
MC

M/L Mitt Right

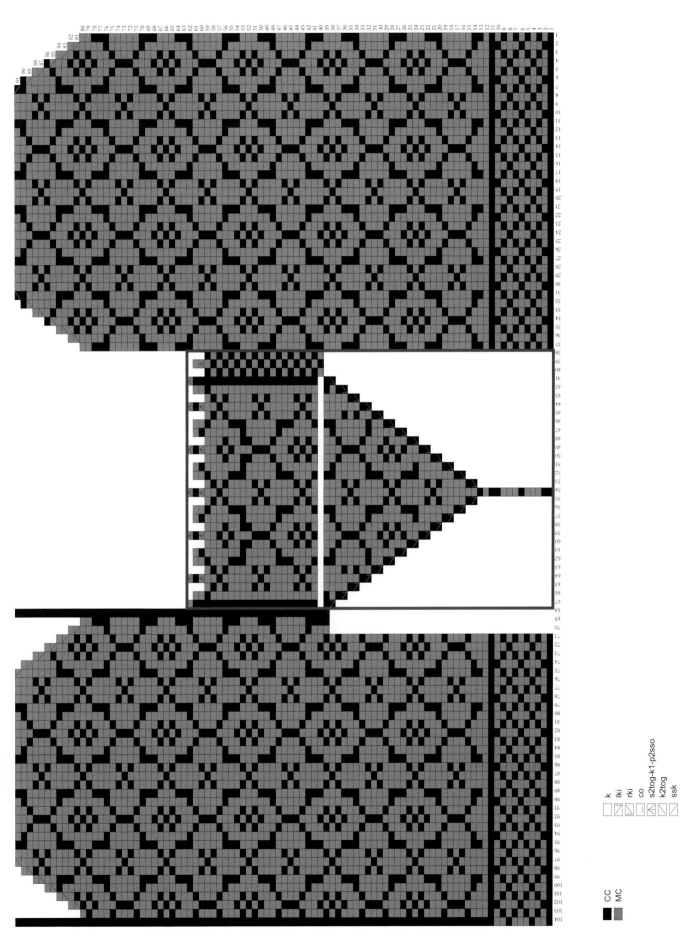

k
lki
rki
co
s2tog-k1-p2sso
k2tog
ssk

CC
MC

QUATREFOIL FULL MITTENS

Size
S/M (M/L), to fit hand circumference 7½ (8½)in / 19 (21.5)cm

Finished Measurements
Hand circumference 8 (9)in / 20.5 (23)cm

Yarn
Impulse of Delight Blue Faced Bliss, 100% Bluefaced Leicester wool, 375 yds / 110g, 1 skein each Alpenglow (MC) and Chocolate Wine (CC).

Needles
US 1½ (2.5mm) circular(s) or double pointed, as preferred, or size to obtain gauge.

Gauge
32 sts and 44 rnds = 4in /10cm in stranded stockinette stitch

Notions & Other Supplies
Yarn needle, 3 stitch markers (one unique for beg of rnd), waste yarn, spare circular for provisional CO (optional).

Required Skills
Knitting in the round, stranded knitting, provisional cast on, sewn hem, chart reading.

Pattern Notes
You can work a plain hem by purling the entire turning round rather than [yo, k2tog].

Picot Hem
Provisionally CO 64 (72) sts in MC. Join in the round, being careful not to twist. PM for beginning of round.
Knit 7 rnds.
Picot rnd: *Yo, k2tog; rep from * to end.
Knit 7 rnds.
Fold cuff with wrong sides facing. If you used waste yarn rather than an extra circular needle for your provisional cast on, place those stitches on a needle now and hold behind the working needle.
Next rnd: *Knit 1 from front needle tog with 1 from back needle; rep from * to end.
Knit 4 rounds in MC.

Remainder of Cuff & Hand
Work Rnds 1-11 of Right or Left Mitten Chart.
Rnd 12:
Right Mitten: Work through stitch 33 (37) as charted, pm for thumb gusset, work 1 as charted, pm for thumb gusset, work to end of round.

Left Mitten: Work through stitch 30 (34) as charted, pm for thumb gusset, work 1 as charted, pm for thumb gusset, work to end of round.

Continue working in pattern, slipping markers as you reach them.

When you have completed the thumb gusset portion of the chart, on the next rnd (chart Rnd 40) place the 27 thumb stitches on waste yarn as indicated, CO 3 sts using the backward loop cast on method, and continue working the rest of the mitten chart. 65 (73) sts.
Work decreases (ssk, k2tog, cdd) in the CC or MC as shown on the chart.
Graft top together using CC.

Thumb
Replace the 27 thumb sts onto your needles. Pick up and knit 3 sts from the edge of the opening then work to end of Rnd 41 as charted. PM for beginning of rnd. 30 sts.
Finish chart, working decreases as charted. Cut yarn and draw CC through rem 7 sts. Pull snugly to close hole.

Finishing
Weave in loose ends. Block.

ABBREVIATIONS

(k, p) in 1: Knit, leaving the stitch on the needle, and then purl into the same stitch.

(k, p, k) in 1: Knit, leaving the stitch on the needle, then purl, and then knit into the same stitch.

(p, k) in 1: Purl, leaving the stitch on the needle, and then knit into the same stitch.

1/1 LC: Slip 1 stitch to cable needle and hold in front; k1; k1 from cable needle.

1/1 LPC: Slip 1 stitch to cable needle and hold in front; p1; k1 from cable needle.

1/1 RC: Slip 1 stitch to cable needle and hold in back; k1; k1 from cable needle.

1/1 RPC: Slip 1 stitch to cable needle and hold in back; k1; p1 from cable needle.

1/1/1 LCpc: Sl 1 to CN, hold in front. K1, p1. K1 from CN.

1/1/1 RCpc: Slip 2 to CN, hold in back. K1. P1, K1 from CN.

1/2 LC: Slip 1 stitch to cable needle and hold in front; k2; k1 from cable needle.

1/2 LPC: Slip 1 stitch to cable needle and hold in front; p2; k1 from cable needle.

1/2 RC: Slip 2 stitches to cable needle and hold in back; k1; k2 from cable needle.

1/2 RPC: Slip 2 stitches to cable needle and hold in back; k1; p2 from cable needle.

beg: Beginning.

BO: Bind off.

cdi: Central double increase. Knit through back loop, then front loop of the same stitch. Lift the vertical strand between the two stitches just created and knit into it.

CC: Contrast color.

CO: Cast on.

cont: Continue(s).

dec: Decrease.

foll: Following; follows.

k tbl: Knit through the back loop.

k: Knit.

k2tog: Knit 2 stitches together.

k3tog: Knit 3 stitches together.

k-tbl: Knit through the back loop.

lki: Lift the stitch 2 rows below the last stitch onto the left needle and knit this stitch.

M1L: From the front, lift the horizontal strand between stitches with the left needle. Knit through the back loop.

M1P: Make one purlwise.

M1R: From the back, lift the horizontal strand between stitches with the left needle. Knit through the front loop.

MC: Main color.

p: Purl.

p2tog: Purl 2 stitches together.

p3tog: Purl 3 stitches together.

patt: Pattern.

PB: Place bead.

pm: Place marker.

p-tbl: url through the back loop.

rem: Remain(s); remaining.

rep: Repeat.

rki : Lift the stitch 1 row below the next stitch onto the left needle and knit this stitch.

rnd(s): Round(s).

RS: Right side.

s1 wyif: With the working yarn in front, insert the right needle into the next stitch as if to purl and transfer the stitch from the left needle to the right.

s1 or sl1wyib: With the working yarn in back, insert the right needle into the next stitch as if to purl and transfer the stitch from the left needle to the right.

s1-k1-psso: Slip one stitch knitwise, then knit next stitch and pass the slipped stitch over.

s1-k2tog-psso (sk2p): Slip one stitch knitwise, then knit 2 stitches together and pass the slipped stitch over.

s2tog-k1-p2sso (s2kp): Slip 2 stitches together knitwise, knit 1, then pass slipped stitches over.

sl: Slip.

sl1-k1-psso (skp): Slip 1 st knitwise, knit 1, then pass slipped stitch over.

sm: Slip marker.

ssk: Slip 2 stitches knitwise, then knit slipped stitches together.

sssk: Slip 3 stitches knitwise, then knit slipped stitches together.

St st: Stockinette stitch.

st(s): Stitches.

tbl: Through the back loop.

tog: Together.

w&t: Wrap & turn.

WS: Wrong side.

wyib: With yarn in back.

wyif: With yarn in front.

yo: Yarnover.

BIBLIOGRAPHY & RESOURCES

California Revival: Vintage Décor for Today's Homes. Carol Coates & Annie Dietz, Schiffer, 2007. This book focuses on small pieces, furniture and architectural details, rather than the overall architecture of the style, though there are plenty of large interior and exterior shots.

California Tile: The Golden Era 1910-1940. Volume 1, *Acme to Handcraft* and Volume 2, *Hispano-Moresque to Woolenius*. Joseph A. Taylor, Ed., The California Heritage Museum, Schiffer, 2004. These two volumes include chapters on, if not all, nearly all the California tile producers in the early 20th century, and thousands of images of tiles, installations, etc.

California Colonial: The Spanish and Rancho Revival Styles. Elizabeth McMilian, Schiffer, 2002. Great historical overview, ranging back to the 1700s and the impact of original work on more recent interpretations of the style.

Red Tile Style: America's Spanish Revival Architecture. Arrol Gellner, Viking Studio, 2002. Not just California. Divided into sections to include Las Casitas to Los Edificios Publicos. Mostly exterior details.

Casa California: Spanish Style Houses from Santa Barbara to San Clemente. Elizabeth McMillian, Rizzoli, 1996. Total eye candy of some of the most famous houses. Primarily exterior shots, but also some interior photographs.

Websites and other resources

Photostream for California Pottery and Tile Works
www.flickr.com/photos/californiapotteryandtileworks

California Potteries website
www.calpot.com

This Old House Los Angeles Project
www.thisoldhouse.com/toh/tv/house-project/overview/0,,20427806,00.html

Martha Stewart Adamson House Tour
http://www.marthastewart.com/275611/home-tour-adamson-house/@center/276999/home-tours

Adamson House wiki
en.wikipedia.org/wiki/Adamson_House

Adamson House website
www.adamsonhouse.org

Yarns Used

Bijou Basin
Bijou Basin Ranch is a small family-owned-and-run yak ranch located just outside the small town of Elbert on the open plains of the Colorado outback about 65 miles southeast of Denver, Colorado. They raise registered full-blooded yaks that have superior glossy coats which are harvested annually. They also supplement the fiber we harvest from their yaks by buying quality yak fiber from other yak ranchers across the country and abroad. The yak fiber is then processed into yarn at various mills across the country or abroad and sold under the Bijou Spun label. www.BijouBasinRanch.com

Black Water Abbey
Marilyn King started Black Water Abbey Yarns after a trip to Ireland where she visited a small mill producing traditional knitting wool. For over a decade Marilyn has imported this "old fashioned knitting wool in really good colors," selling directly to knitters through her website. In addition she has sourced patterns and buttons that complement the yarn, and has recently begun to create more original designs. It is probably not a surprise to learn that Marilyn loves cable knitting. www.abbeyyarns.com

Blue Sky Alpacas
Blue Sky Alpacas' yarn lines include go-to classics, exquisite specialty fibers and crave-worthy organic cottons, with a focus on soft and decadent alpaca. blueskyalpacas.com

Dragonfly Fibers
Dragonfly Fibers is an indie yarn company specializing in artisan dyed yarn. The "colors of happiness" are created and shared with the world by Kate Chiocchio and the amazing Team Dragonfly—made up mostly of friends based in the Washington, DC, area. Find the yarns online, in brick and mortar yarn shops across the country, as well as at various fiber festivals throughout the year. www.dragonflyfibers.com

Elemental Affects
Jeane de Coster founded Elemental Affects in 2005, specializing in domestic fiber. (Her first yarns were from the largest flock of Shetland sheep in the US.) She especially loves dyeing over naturally colored yarn. www.elementalaffects.com

Hazel Knits
Hazel Knits is the brainchild and consuming passion of Seattleite Wendee Shulsen. Working part-time at a local yarn shop, Wendee realized there was an unsatisfied demand for more color and yarn options. After experimenting on her own and loving the results, she went into business in 2007 and currently offers a full line of original colorways on custom-milled stock. When she's not in the studio perfecting her next creation, Wendee spends her free time hanging precariously from rock walls, sleeping under the stars, and nibbling on figs and goat cheese. www.hazelknits.com

Impulse of Delight
Ruth has rarely encountered a textile pursuit she didn't want to try—she knits constantly, crochets occasionally, and is presently hooked on weaving, not to mention her hand-dyed yarn business. She adores color, and finds macro nature photography to be a marvelous exercise in mindfulness, as well as a source of creative inspiration. www.impulse-of-delight.com

Jamieson's
Jamieson's Shetland wools are grown and uniquely spun on Shetland, a group of islands in the North Sea, Scotland. Their yarns, including Shetland Sprindrift with over 220 colors, are distributed in North America by Simply Shetland. Visit www.simplyshetland.com for a list of stores.

Knit Picks
Knit Picks is an online yarn supplied passionately committed to affordable luxury knitting and crochet. Visit KnitPicks.com for a wide selection of natural fiber yarns, and much more.

Little Red Bicycle
Little Red Bicycle is a small, independent dyeworks located in the San Francisco Bay Area. In the LRB studio they believe in producing addictive color, whether it's in-your-face bright or calm and calculated. Each customer is considered a friend, so come knit with them! www.littleredbicycle.com

MacKintosh Yarns

MacKintosh Yarns was founded in July 2007 in Iowa City, Iowa, by Elizabeth Bernstein. The company takes its name from Elizabeth's Australian Shepherd of the same name, MacKintosh, also known as Mac. Elizabeth has been knitting since the age of seven. Her passion for color and fiber is why she strives to produce the highest quality luxury hand-painted yarns and spinning fibers available in so many scrumptious colors. www.macyarns.com

Sanguine Gryphon

The Wrought socks are shown in Adonis Blue 'Bugga!' yarn originating from The Sanguine Gryphon. 'Bugga!' is now available at two new independent yarn companies, The Verdant Gryphon (www.verdantgryphon.com) and Cephalopod Yarns (www.cephalopodyarns.com). Requests for the colorway shown should be directed to Cephalopod Yarns.

Shibui Knits

Shibui Knits is based in Portland, Oregon, a city that is internationally famous for creativity and the arts. *Shibui* means "elegant with a touch of bitterness" in Japanese, and they try to bring that sentiment to all of their products. Their current selection of yarns have been spun from the finest fibers available, then dyed in their special color palette. The result is a breadth of both color and texture, creating yarns that are both beautiful to look at and luxurious to touch. www.shibuiknits.com

Stricken Smitten

Stricken Smitten specializes in small batches of luxury yarns dyed in layered semi-solid colorways. Désirée lives and dyes in Seattle where she is overjoyed to spend her days spilling things. Find Stricken Smitten yarn at www.strickensmitten.com and The Loopy Ewe.

Woolen Rabbit

Kim Kaslow, owner of The Woolen Rabbit, is a small, independent dyer located in the White Mountains of New Hampshire. Color has always been her passion and she has been slowly building her business over the last ten years, while working a full-time job. It has always been important to her to keep her business small enough so that it would never feel like work, but big enough that she would be able to give up her full time job someday. www.thewoolenrabbit.com

These companies supplied beads & buttons for the book:

Bead Wrangler: www.7beads.com
JHB International, Inc: www.buttons.com

ABOUT STEPHANNIE TALLENT

Stephannie lives in Hermosa Beach, California, with husband Dave, dog Rigel and Tonkinese cats Meggie, Obi and Cali.

She's been knitting on and off for the past 30-plus years, and began publishing her knitting designs several years ago. Her favorite techniques include cables, Bavarian twisted stitches and stranded knitting.

She also tech edits.

When she's not designing, knitting, tech editing or working as a veterinarian, she gardens (native plants and vegetables), hikes, and beach-combs. She blogs at www.sunsetcat.com. Find her on Ravelry as Stephcat.

ABOUT COOPERATIVE PRESS

Cooperative Press (formerly anezka media) was founded in 2007 by Shannon Okey, a voracious reader as well as writer and editor, who had been doing freelance acquisitions work, introducing authors with projects she believed in to editors at various publishers.

Although working with traditional publishers can be very rewarding, there are some books that fly under their radar. They're too avant–garde, or the marketing department doesn't know how to sell them, or they don't think they'll sell 50,000 copies in a year.

5,000 or 50,000. Does the book matter to that 5,000? Then it should be published.

In 2009, Cooperative Press changed its named to reflect the relationships we have developed with authors working on books. We work together to put out the best quality books we can and share in the proceeds accordingly.

Thank you for supporting independent publishers and authors.

http://www.cooperativepress.com